Shogi
将棋
A Complete Guide to Japanese Customs and Culture
Chess
チェス
bee / PIXTA（ピクスタ）
➡P46

Bonsai

盆栽

A Complete Guide to *Japanese* Customs and Culture

➡P92

Potted plants
西洋式の鉢植え植物
JayTurbo / PIXTA（ピクスタ）
➡P 2

A Complete Guide to
Japanese
Customs and Culture
迎春
Osechi
お節
P190
june. / PIXTA（ピクスタ）

Dishes for Thanksgiving
感謝祭の料理
Rawpixel / PIXTA（ピクスタ）
➡P190

→P226

A Complete Guide to
Japanese
Customs and Culture
London
ロンドン
samot / PIXTA（ピクスタ）
➡P226

Shamisen
三味線

A Complete Guide to
Japanese
Customs and Culture

Guitar
ギター

➡P20

英語でガイド！

世界とくらべてわかる
日本まるごと紹介事典

江口 裕之 著

Jリサーチ出版

　今や日本文化が世界中でブームです。日本を訪れる外国人は年々増え続け、皆さんの中にも日本の様々な側面を英語で説明する機会が増えた方も多いのではないでしょうか。そのような場面において、特に最近では、説明をする相手が必ずしも英語圏の方とは限らなくなりました。英語を第二言語、第三言語として用いておられる方も多く、その文化的背景も様々です。そのような場合、英語表現はできるだけ簡潔なほうが通じやすいですし、説明も具体的なイメージが沸きやすい内容が求められます。

　例えば、「お好み焼きってどんな食べ物？」と聞かれて、どこから説明してよいやら迷うかもしれませんが、そんな時に便利なアプローチは、外国にも存在する、似たような食べ物を挙げることです。お好み焼きは、よくpancake（パンケーキ）と説明されますが、確かに、どちらも小麦粉を水で溶いたものをベースにしているので似ています。ところが、食べてみると全く違うものであることが分かります。pancake が甘いのに対し、お好み焼きは甘くありません。さらに、pancake がスナック感覚で食されるのに対し、お好み焼きは食事という感覚です。その点からすると、お好み焼きは、pizza（ピザ）に近いのかもしれません。

　他愛もないトリビアのように聞こえるかもしれませんが、実は奥が深いところなのです。お好み焼きと pancake のような、異文化間における似たような事象の比較を通じて、それらの事象そのものや、背景にある文化的な違いがよりよく理解できるようになりますし、また、それらの類似点・相違点を明確に伝える英語表現を知ることにより、語彙力や説明力の幅が広くなります。このような比較は、日本文化を英語で説明したい方々にとって、魅力的な学習分野ではないでしょうか。そのように考え、今回、筆を執ることにいたしました。

　本書では、先の「お好み焼き VS. Pancakes」のような構図で、日本に関する 125 の事象を扱います。着物や相撲などの伝統文化、折り紙や居酒屋などの生活文化、忍者や新幹線のような観光地での話題、カラオケやマンガのようなポップカルチャー、さらには、国会や自衛隊などの日本の政治・社会に関する話題も含まれています。それらを5つの分野に大別して、それぞれの簡潔な説明を紹介し、その後に、外国の似たような、あるいは、相反するような事象を取り上げ、質疑応答の形で比較してみました。中には、「すし」や「歌舞伎」など、もう少し知りたい、という項目もあります。それらについては、各分野から5本をピックアップして、追加のページを割き、質疑応答の続編を掲載してあります。

　基本的に、英語表現はできる限り簡潔にしたつもりですが、質疑応答やその続編においては、チャレンジの気持ちも含めて、やや高度な表現を織り交ぜた部分もあります。知らない表現などが出てきた場合、得をした気持ちで、自分でも使えるように習得していただければと思います。

　私自身、これまで英語による日本文化紹介の本を数多く書かせていただいていますが、本書の執筆を通じて、新しい発見が数多くあり、楽しく、また、チャレンジングな気持ちで取り組ませていただきました。中には、複数の説があるものや、まだ説が存在しないものもあります。そのような場合は、自分の主観に頼りましたが、私の経験から、外国の方に十分に納得していただける説明になったと自負しております。日本文化を英語で紹介したい方々に、本書のアプローチが新しい視点を提供することができれば、それに勝る喜びはございません。

　最後に、本書の執筆にあたって、様々な提案や協力をいただいた、Ｊリサーチ出版編集部の鈴木 郁さんに、この場を借りて、御礼申し上げます。

江口裕之

目次　CONTENTS

本書の使い方

まずはそれぞれのトピックについて学びましょう。日本の文化や習慣について、英語で説明できるようにくり返し練習しましょう。

006 Shamisen
三味線

What is shamisen?

Shamisen is a traditional Japanese musical instrument similar to a guitar. It has three strings, and is played with a pick shaped like a spatula. The shamisen is used to accompany traditional Japanese folk songs and bunraku narrations. There are several different types depending on the neck size.

訳 三味線って何だろう？
三味線は、伝統的な和楽器で、ギターに似ています。三味線には 3 本の弦があり、ヘラのような形のピックで弾きます。三味線は、伝統的な日本の民謡や文楽の語りの伴奏に用いられます。棹の太さによって、いくつかの種類があります。

イラストで くらべる！

Shamisen 三味線 **VS** Guitar ギター

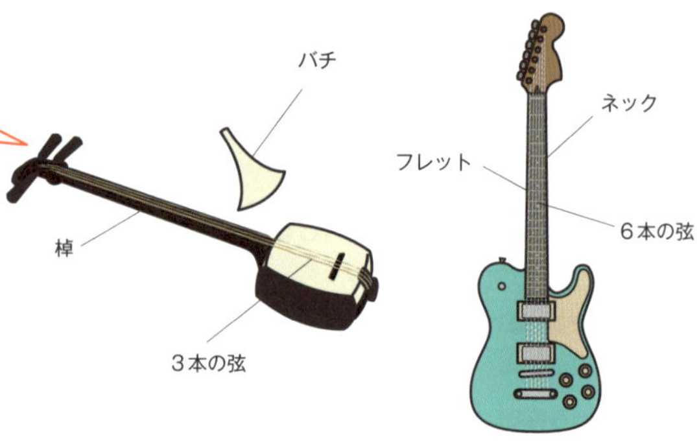

20

日本と海外の似ているものについて、イラストや写真で比べてみましょう。

※斜体になっている単語は、リーダーズ英和辞典、リーダーズプラス、ジーニアス英和大辞典、ランダムハウス英和大辞典、オックスフォード新英英辞典、オックスフォード米語辞典、オックスフォード現代英英辞典、ロングマン現代英英辞典のいずれの辞書にもエントリーのないものです。

くらべて スッキリ!

 Shamisen を英語で説明してみよう

Q. **What are some differences between the guitar and the shamisen?**

ギターと三味線はどう違うの？

A. The biggest difference is that the shamisen uses animal skins for the resonator surface, so its mechanism is more like that of a banjo. Also, the shamisen neck doesn't have frets, and has a part that intentionally touches the thickest string, which creates a distinctive distortion sound.

最大の違いは、三味線が共鳴器の表面に動物の皮を張っているとこで、仕組みとしてはバンジョーに近いね。それに、三味線のネック（棹）にはフレットがないし、一番太い弦に意図的に触るように作られた部分があって、そこが独特の歪んだような音を作り出すんだ。

> 日本と海外の似ているものについて、詳しく解説しています。Q & A 形式で楽しく読み進めることができます。

> 本文で扱ったボキャブラリーです。辞書なしでどんどん読み進めることができます。

🎎 Vocabulary 語句

musical instrument	楽器	animal skin	動物の皮
string	名 弦	resonator	名 共鳴器
pick	名 ピック（弦楽器の弦をはじくための爪で、plectrum とも）	mechanism	名 仕組み
spatula	名 ヘラ（絵具を伸ばしたり、膏薬を伸ばしたりするときに用いる）	banjo	名 バンジョー（4弦あるいは5弦の楽器で、共鳴器の表面にドラムヘッドを取り付けた楽器）
accompany	動 ～の伴奏をする	fret	名 フレット（ギターの指板に打ち込まれた音程を決めるための金属）
folk song	民謡	intentionally	副 意図的に
narration	名 語り	distortion sound	歪んだ音
neck	名 （弦楽器）のネック（三味線の場合は「棹」と呼ばれる）		

音声ダウンロードの手順

STEP 1 商品ページにアクセス！　方法は次の3通り！

① 右のコードを読み取ってアクセス。

② https://www.jresearch.co.jp/book/b372859.html を
入力してアクセス。

③ Ｊリサーチ出版のホームページ
（https://www.jresearch.co.jp/）にアクセスして、
「キーワード」に書籍名を入れて検索。

STEP 2 ページ内にある「音声ダウンロード」
ボタンをクリック！

STEP 3 ユーザー名「1001」、パスワード「24000」を入力！

STEP 4 音声の利用方法は2通り！
学習スタイルに合わせた方法でお聴きください！

1
「音声ファイル一括ダウンロード」より、
ファイルをダウンロードして聴く。

2
▶ボタンを押して、その場で再生して聴く。

※ダウンロードした音声ファイルは、パソコン・スマートフォンなどでお聴きいただくことができます。一括ダウンロードの音声ファイルは .zip 形式で圧縮してあります。解凍してご利用ください。ファイルの解凍がうまくできない場合は、直接の音声再生も可能です。

音声ダウンロードについてのお問合せ先：
toiawase@jresearch.co.jp（受付時間：平日9時〜18時）

文化
Culture

Ukiyo-e

浮世絵

What is ukiyo-e?

Ukiyo-e is a genre of pictures depicting the lives of the commoners during the Edo Period. Typical subjects of ukiyo-e included beautiful women, kabuki actors and landscapes. Because ukiyo-e were mostly made by woodblock printing, they were mass-produced, making them affordable for the commoners as a casual form of entertainment.

浮世絵って何だろう？

浮世絵は、江戸時代の庶民の生活を描いた絵の分野です。典型的な画題は美人女性、歌舞伎役者、風景などです。浮世絵は、ほとんどが木版画で作製されていたため大量生産され、手軽な娯楽の一形式として、庶民でも手が届くものでした。

イラストで **くらべる！**

Ukiyo-e 浮世絵 **VS** **Western painting** 西洋画

遠近法を取らない　　　　　　　　遠近法に注目

木版画　　　　　　　　　　　　　写実的
大量生産

くらべてスッキリ！

Ukiyo-e を英語で説明してみよう

Q. How do you compare ukiyo-e and the Western paintings of the time?

浮世絵を当時の西洋画と比べるとどう？

A. Western paintings in those days try to depict objects and people realistically, focusing on perspective, shade and shadow. In contrast, ukiyo-e clearly depicts their outlines, using no shadow or shade. Such unique aspects of ukiyo-e greatly influenced Western painters of the time, especially impressionist artists like Van Gogh.

当時の西洋画は、遠近や陰影に注目して、物体や人を写実的に描こうとするけど、これとは対照的に、浮世絵はそれらの輪郭を明確に描いて、陰影は使わないんだ。そんな浮世絵の独特な側面が、当時の西洋の画家、特にゴッホのような印象派の芸術家たちに大きな影響を与えたんだ。

Vocabulary 語句

genre	名 ジャンル、部門、分野（genre には「風俗画」の意味もある）
depict	動 ～を描く
the commoners	庶民（特に身分階級が存在した江戸時代の庶民を指す）
typical	形 典型的な
subject	名 画題
landscape	名 風景
woodblock printing	木版画
mass-produce	動 ～を大量生産する
affordable	形 手の届く
casual	形 手軽な
entertainment	名 娯楽
realistically	副 写実的に
perspective	名 遠近（法）
shade and shadow	陰影
outline	名 輪郭
impressionist	形 印象派の

Rakugo

落語

What is *rakugo*?

Rakugo is traditional comic storytelling performed solo. A *rakugo-ka* sits on a zabuton cushion placed on the stage, and speaks all the dialogues of the characters in the story, using different voice tones and gestures. Many *rakugo* stories focus on everyday lives of the commoners during the Edo Period.

落語って何だろう？

落語は、独りで滑稽な物語を話す伝統的な芸です。落語家は、舞台に置かれた座布団に座り、異なる口調や身振りを使い分け、登場人物のすべてのセリフを語ります。落語の物語は、多くが江戸時代の庶民の日常生活に焦点を当てています。

イラストで くらべる！

Rakugo を英語で説明してみよう

Q. **How do you compare *rakugo* with stand-up comedy?**

落語とスタンドアップコメディを比べるとどう？

A. **There are no set rules for stand-up comedy, but in *rakugo* there are many restrictions. For example, *rakugo-ka* remain sitting during their performance and use only a hand towel and a folding fan as stage props. Because of such restrictions, however, *rakugo-ka* and their audience can fully use imagination.**

スタンドアップコメディには決まったルールはないけど、落語にはいろんな制限があるんだ。例えば、落語家は上演中は座ったままだし、小道具も手拭と扇子だけしか使わない。でも、そんな制限があるからこそ、落語家も観客も想像力を大いに働かせることができるんだ。

🎎 Vocabulary 語句

comic	形 滑稽な		focus on 〜	〜に焦点を当てる
storytelling	名 物語を話すこと		the commoners	庶民（特に身分階級が存在した江戸時代の庶民を指す）
performed solo	1人で演じられる			
dialogue	名 会話			
character	名 登場人物		restriction	名 制限
voice tone	口調		stage prop	小道具
gesture	名 身振り		imagination	名 想像力

Bunraku

文楽

What is bunraku?

Bunraku is traditional Japanese puppet theater. It developed in the Edo Period and became popular among the commoners. Three puppeteers manipulate one puppet, and a narrator called *tayu* delivers stories and dialogues to the accompaniment of the shamisen. Bunraku stories deal with legendary heroes and romance.

訳 文楽って何だろう？　文楽は、伝統的な日本の人形劇です。文楽は、江戸時代に発達し、庶民の間で人気になりました。3人の人形遣いが1つの人形を操り、太夫と呼ばれる語り手が、三味線の伴奏に合わせて、物語とセリフを語ります。文楽の物語は、伝説的英雄や恋愛を扱っています。

イラストで **くらべる！**

Bunraku 文楽　VS　Western puppet theater 西洋の人形劇

人形遣い（観客に見えている）

人形遣い（顔は見えない）

糸で吊るしたり、背後や舞台下から操作するものがある

Bunraku を英語で説明してみよう

Q. **How is bunraku different from Western puppet theater?**

文楽は、西洋の人形劇とどう違うの？

A. **Western puppet theater is for children, and is small in scale, whereas bunraku is for an adult audience, often dealing with love stories, and the puppets are much bigger, with the heights of 130 to 150 cm. Also, puppeteers are visible to the audience, and some famous puppeteers perform unhooded.**

西洋の人形劇は、子供向けで規模も小さいけど、文楽は大人向けで、恋愛物などを扱うことも多く、人形もはるかに大きくて、背丈が 130cm から 150cm ほどもあるよ。それに人形遣いは観客から見えるし、有名な人形遣いは、顔を隠さずに上演するね。

Vocabulary　語句

puppet theater	人形劇（**puppet** は「人形」、**theater** は「演劇」の意味）	**to the accompaniment of ～**	～の伴奏に合わせて
		deal with ～	～を扱う
the commoners	庶民（身分階級がある社会における庶民を指す）	**legendary hero**	伝説的英雄
		romance	名 恋愛
puppeteer	名 人形遣い	**audience**	名 観客
manipulate	動 ～を操る	**visible to ～**	～から見える
narrator	名 語り手	**unhooded**	形 顔を隠さずに（「フード（**hood**）、覆い」を「付けないで」の意味）
deliver	動 （歌、詩、物語、会話などを）語る		
dialogue	名 対話、セリフ		

Noh
能

004

What is noh?

Noh is a classical form of stage art which developed in the Middle Ages and became popular among samurai. It is characterized by the highly stylized movements of the actors, the masks worn by the main actors, and the distinctive narrative chants accompanied by an orchestra of flutes and drums.

能って何だろう？
能は、古典的な舞台芸能で、中世に発達し武士の間で人気になりました。能は、高度に形式化した役者の動き、主役が付ける面、笛と太鼓の伴奏による独特の謡が特徴です。

Noh mask 能面 VS Western mask 西洋のマスク

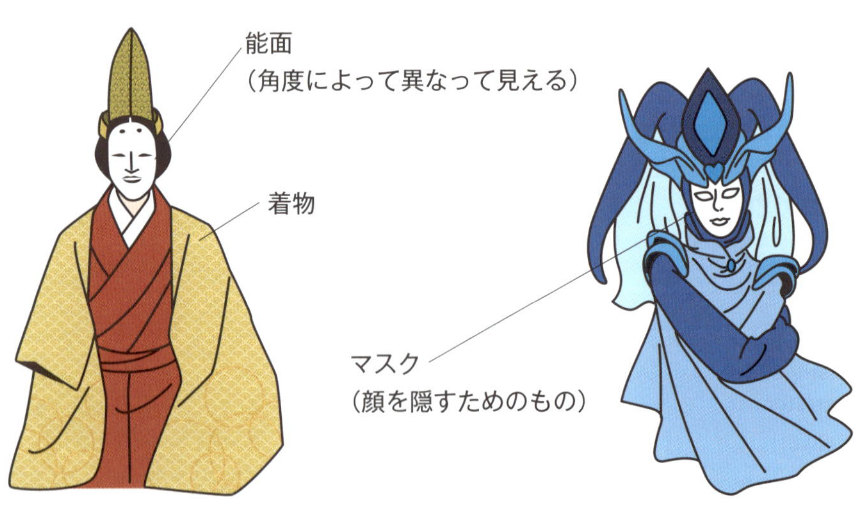

Noh masks を英語で説明してみよう

Q. **How do you compare noh masks and Western masks?**

能面と西洋のマスクを比べるとどう？

A. In the West, masks are basically to hide the wearers' faces, as used in masquerade balls, but noh masks are to transform the wearers into other selves, including supernatural beings. Another characteristic is that noh masks are so designed that the facial expressions look different according to their angle.

西洋ではマスクというと、仮面舞踏会で使われているように、基本的に着用する人の顔を隠すためのものだよね。でも能面は、着用する人を、超自然物を含め、別の存在に変身させるためのものなんだ。もう１つの特徴は、能面は角度によって表情が異なって見えるように作られていることだね。

🎎 Vocabulary 語句

noh	能（**no** とも綴られるが、誤解を避けるために **h** を入れるのが普通。また、多くの英英辞書では **Noh** のように固有名詞的に **N** を大文字にしているが、ここでは **kabuki**、**kyogen**、**bunraku** と同列扱いで **n** を小文字にしてある）
classical	形 古典的な
stage art	舞台芸能
stylized	形 形式化した

distinctive	形 独特な
narrative	形 語るような
chant	名 詠唱、単調に歌うこと
accompanied by ～	～で伴奏された
orchestra	名 楽団
hide	動 ～を隠す
masquerade ball	仮面舞踏会
transform A into B	A を B に変身させる
supernatural being	超自然物
facial expression	表情

Kyogen
狂言

What is kyogen?

Kyogen is a form of comical theater, which developed in the Middle Ages. It is usually performed in between Noh plays. Kyogen stories satirically and humorously describe the upper class people from the commoners' viewpoint. Kyogen actors also perform an interlude of a noh play to explain the story.

狂言って何だろう？　狂言は、滑稽な演劇の様式で、中世に発達しました。狂言は通常、能の出し物の間に演じられます。狂言の物語は、上流階級の人たちを庶民の観点から皮肉を込めて面白く描きます。狂言師はまた、能の物語を説明するために、能の幕間劇も演じます。

イラストで **くらべる！**

Kyogen を英語で説明してみよう

Q. Is kyogen like a comedy theater?

狂言って、コメディ演劇みたいなもの？

A. **Yes, it is, but since it has a long history, the performing style is very traditional and highly stylized, featuring distinctive voices and movements. The stories are comical, but tend to be critical of the upper classes, often describing people paying the price for their arrogance in the end.**

そうだね。でも歴史が長いので、演じ方はとても伝統的で、すごく形式化していて、独特な声や動きが特徴だね。物語は滑稽なんだけど、上流階級に対して批判的な傾向があって、最後には自分の傲慢さの代償を払うような内容が多いね。

🟥 Vocabulary 語句

comical	形 滑稽な		interlude	名 幕間劇（独立した演目の本狂言とは別に、能の幕間にその物語の背景などを説明するために演じられる間狂言のこと）
theater	名 演劇（この意味では不可算名詞）			
in between ~	~の間に		explain	動 ~を説明する
satirically	副 皮肉を込めて		stylized	形 形式化した
humorously	副 面白く		distinctive	形 独特の
describe	動 ~を描く		critical of ~	~に批判的な
the upper class people	上流階級の人たち		pay the price for ~	~の代償を払う
from the commoners' viewpoint	庶民の観点から		arrogance	名 傲慢さ

Shamisen

三味線

What is shamisen?

Shamisen is a traditional Japanese musical instrument similar to a guitar. It has three strings, and is played with a pick shaped like a spatula. The shamisen is used to accompany traditional Japanese folk songs and bunraku narrations. There are several different types depending on the neck size.

三味線って何だろう？

三味線は、伝統的な和楽器で、ギターに似ています。三味線には 3 本の弦があり、ヘラのような形のピックで弾きます。三味線は、伝統的な日本の民謡や文楽の語りの伴奏に用いられます。棹の太さによって、いくつかの種類があります。

イラストで **くらべる！**

Shamisen 三味線 **VS** Guitar ギター

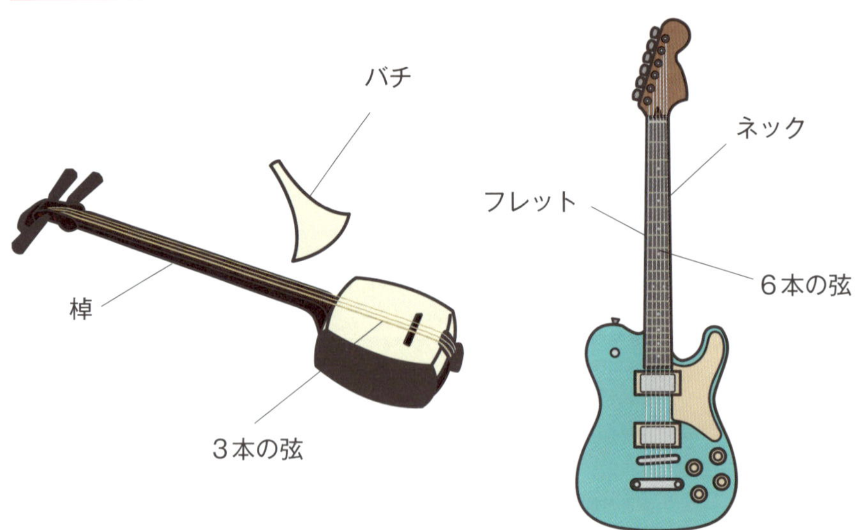

Shamisen を英語で説明してみよう

Q. What are some differences between the guitar and the shamisen?

ギターと三味線はどう違うの？

A. The biggest difference is that the shamisen uses animal skins for the resonator surface, so its mechanism is more like that of a banjo. Also, the shamisen neck doesn't have frets, and has a part that intentionally touches the thickest string, which creates a distinctive distortion sound.

最大の違いは、三味線が共鳴器の表面に動物の皮を張っているとこで、仕組みとしてはバンジョーに近いね。それに、三味線のネック（棹）にはフレットがないし、一番太い弦に意図的に触るように作られた部分があって、そこが独特の歪んだような音を作り出すんだ。

🟤 Vocabulary 語句

musical instrument	楽器
string	名 弦
pick	名 ピック（弦楽器の弦をはじくための爪で、**plectrum** とも）
spatula	名 ヘラ（絵具を伸ばしたり、膏薬を伸ばしたりするときに用いる）
accompany	動 〜の伴奏をする
folk song	民謡
narration	名 語り
neck	名 （弦楽器）のネック（三味線の場合は「棹」と呼ばれる）

animal skin	動物の皮
resonator	名 共鳴器
mechanism	名 仕組み
banjo	名 バンジョー（4弦あるいは5弦の楽器で、共鳴器の表面にドラムヘッドを取り付けた楽器）
fret	名 フレット（ギターの指板に打ち込まれた音程を決めるための金属）
intentionally	副 意図的に
distortion sound	歪んだ音

Wadaiko

和太鼓

What is *wadaiko*?

Wadaiko are traditional Japanese drums. They vary according to their uses. Shallow ones are placed on a stand and played with sticks. A large, deep-bodied one is placed horizontally on a stand, and can be played from both sides. Small drums called *tsuzumi* are held on the shoulder or the knee and played with fingers.

和太鼓って何だろう？　和太鼓は、伝統的な日本の太鼓です。和太鼓は、用途によって様々です。胴が短い和太鼓は台座に置いてバチで打ちます。大きくて胴が長い太鼓は、台座に水平に置き、両面から演奏することもできます。鼓と呼ばれる小さなものは、肩か膝にのせて指で打ちます。

イラストで くらべる！

Wadaiko 和太鼓　**VS**　**Western drums** 西洋のドラム

Wadaiko を英語で説明してみよう

Q. **Do you play *wadaiko* just like Western drums?**

和太鼓って、西洋のドラムのように打つの？

A. **As for the small ones, the stick work is quite similar, although unlike Western drums, you don't use your feet. When you play a large drum called *odaiko*, you use very thick sticks, so you need more power. You beat the head from a standing position, using your whole body to generate power.**

小型の和太鼓なら、バチさばきはよく似ているね。もちろん、西洋のドラムと違って、足は使わないけどね。大太鼓と呼ばれる大きな太鼓を打つときは、とても太いスティックを使うから、もっと力がいるよ。力が出るように、立った姿勢から全身を使って太鼓面を打つんだ。

🎎 Vocabulary 語句

use	名 用途	horizontally	副 水平に
shallow	形 薄い（ここでは、太鼓の胴が短いという意味）	shoulder	名 肩
		knee	名 膝
stand	名 台座	stick work	スティックさばき、バチさばき
stick	名 （太鼓の）バチ、（ドラムの）スティック	thick	形 太い
		head	名 ヘッド（ドラムや太鼓の打面）
deep-bodied	形 胴が深い（ここでは、太鼓の胴が長いという意味）		

Geisha
芸者

What is geisha?

Geisha are traditional female entertainers. They wear kimono and a distinctive white makeup. They are dispatched to exclusive traditional restaurants upon request, and entertain the guests by pouring drinks, singing, dancing and playing games with them. Apprentice young geisha are called maiko, who accompany full-fledged geisha.

芸者って何だろう？ 　芸者は、伝統的な女性の芸人です。着物を着て独特の白い化粧をしています。芸者は、求めに応じて高級料亭などに派遣され、客にお酒を注いだり、歌ったり、踊ったり、客と遊びをしたりしてもてなします。見習いの若い芸者は舞妓と呼ばれ、一人前の芸者に付き添います。

イラストで  くらべる！

Geisha 芸者 VS Courtesan 高級娼婦

プロの芸人

遊女

Geisha を英語で説明してみよう

Q. **Geisha are often depicted as courtesans in Western movies. Are they different?**

西洋の映画では、芸者はしばしば高級娼婦のように描かれているけど、実際は違う？

A. **Yes, they are. Geisha are not prostitutes, but professional entertainers. Westerners often confuse geisha with oiran. Oiran were high-class prostitutes in pleasure quarters that once existed in Japan. Oiran were also well-versed in singing, dancing and other cultural arts, so some movie producers must have confused them with geisha.**

うん、違うね。芸者は遊女ではなくてプロの芸人なんだ。西洋人は、よく芸者と花魁を混同するんだ。花魁は、かつて日本に存在した遊郭の高級遊女だったんだ。花魁もまた、歌や踊りなどの文化的な芸事に精通していたから、映画のプロデューサーには花魁を芸者と混同した人たちもいたはずだよ。

🟥 Vocabulary 語句

entertainer	名 芸人
distinctive	形 独特の
dispatch	動 〜を派遣する
exclusive traditional restaurant	高級料亭（飲食物を仕出しで賄うところは茶屋と呼ばれる）
upon request	求めに応じて
apprentice	形 見習いの（芸者は主に関東の名称で、その見習いは半玉と呼ばれる。一方、関西では、芸者は芸妓と呼ばれ、その見習いが舞妓になるが、英語では、混乱を避けるために、芸者・芸妓を geisha、半玉・舞妓を maiko で統一してある）
accompany	動 〜に付き添う
full-fledged	形 一人前の
courtesan	名 高級娼婦
prostitute	名 遊女、売春婦、女郎
pleasure quarter	遊郭（官許の女郎屋が集まっている地域、日本では 1958 年に消滅）
well-versed in 〜	〜に精通して

Kimono

着物

What is kimono?

Kimono is traditional Japanese clothing. It's a kind of robe, folded in front and fastened at the back with a thick sash called an obi. Today, kimono is mainly worn on traditional occasions such as a tea gathering. With an increased interest in Japanese culture, kimono is now regaining popularity.

着物って何だろう？　着物は、伝統的な日本の衣服です。ゆったりとした上着の一種で、前で合わせて、帯と呼ばれる厚い飾り帯を使って後ろで結び留めます。今日、着物は主に、茶会などの伝統的な行事で着用されます。日本文化への関心の高まりとともに、着物が今、人気を取り戻しつつあります。

イラストで くらべる！

Kimono 着物（羽織袴）　VS　Tuxedo タキシード

Kimono を英語で説明してみよう

Q. **Is there a very formal version of kimono, equivalent to a tuxedo in the West?**

西洋のタキシードに相当するような、すごくフォーマルな着物ってあるの？

A. **Yes, there is. It is called haori-hakama. Haori is a jacket worn over a kimono. It often bears the wearer's family crests. Hakama are pleated, loose-fitted trousers. Haori-hakama is worn by men at traditional wedding ceremonies and by boys at the Shichi-go-san ceremony celebrating their growth.**

うん、あるよ。羽織袴と呼ばれている。羽織は着物の上に着る上着で、しばしば着る人の家紋がのっているね。袴は、ゆったりとしたプリーツが付いたズボン。羽織袴は、伝統的な結婚式で男性が着たり、子供の成長を祝う七五三の儀式で男の子が着たりするよ。

🎎 Vocabulary　語句

clothing	名 衣服		tea gathering	茶会
robe	名 ゆったりとした上着、ローブ		regain popularity	人気を取り戻す
			equivalent to ～	～に相当する
fold	動 ～をとじる、ここでは、（着物の前を）合わせる		tuxedo	名 タキシード
			bear	動 ～が描かれている
fasten	動 ～を結び留める		family crest	家紋
sash	名 飾り帯、サッシュ		pleated	形 プリーツ（ひだ）のある
occasion	名 行事		loose-fitted	形 ゆったりとした

Chanoyu

茶の湯

What is chanoyu?

Chanoyu is the art of serving and receiving tea, where the host entertains the guests with the utmost hospitality, while the guests convey their appreciation to the host. Chanoyu was perfected by a tea master, Sen-no-Rikyu, in the 16th century. Chanoyu is regarded as a way to acquire good manners.

訳 茶の湯って何だろう？　茶の湯は、お茶を出したり、いただいたりするための技能です。茶の湯では主人が客人を最高のおもてなしの心で接待する一方、客人は主人に感謝の気持ちを伝えます。茶の湯は、16世紀に茶の大家である千利休によって完成されました。礼儀作法を身につける方法と考えられています。

イラストで **くらべる！**

Chanoyu 茶の湯　VS　Afternoon tea アフタヌーン・ティー

茶器

紅茶

Chanoyu を英語で説明してみよう

Q. **Chanoyu is similar to afternoon tea in England, isn't it?**

茶の湯って、英国のアフタヌーン・ティーに似ているよね？

A. **Yes, it is. Both are a way for people to socialize while enjoying tea and food in proper manners, but chanoyu is more formalized. Also, chanoyu schools have licensing systems; so would-be teachers practice hard to learn about the manners, skills and utensils.**

そうだね。どちらも、正しい作法でお茶や食べ物をいただきながら、社交をする方法だからね。でも茶の湯のほうがもっと儀式化しているね。それに、茶の湯の流派には免状制度があって、茶の湯の先生を目指す人は、作法や技術や茶器などについて懸命に稽古するんだ。

🧧 Vocabulary 語句

art	名 ここでは、技能		master	名 大家
serve	動 〜を出す		good manners	礼儀作法
receive	動 〜をいただく		socialize	動 社交する
host	名 ここでは、主人		proper	形 正しい
utmost	形 最高の		formalized	形 儀式化した
hospitality	名 おもてなしの心		school	名 ここでは、流派
convey A to B	A を B に伝える		would-be 〜	〜を志望する人
appreciation	名 感謝の気持ち		utensil	名 ここでは、茶道具
perfect	動 〜を完成させる			

Ikebana

生け花

What is ikebana?

Ikebana is Japanese flower arrangement. It originated as a way to offer flowers to Buddhist altars, and later developed into a form of decorative art. The basic idea of ikebana is to create a form symbolizing the harmony between man and nature. Many people practice ikebana as a means of self-discipline.

生け花って何だろう？　生け花は日本式のフラワーアレンジメントです。生け花は、仏壇に花を供える方法として発祥し、後に装飾芸術へと発達しました。生け花の基本的な概念は、人と自然の調和を象徴する形を作り出すことです。自己鍛錬の手法として生け花を稽古する人も多くいます。

Ikebana 生け花　VS　Flower arrangement フラワーアレンジメント

芸術作品

室内装飾

Ikebana を英語で説明してみよう

Q. **How is ikebana different from Western flower arrangement?**

生け花は西洋のフラワーアレンジメントとどう違う？

A. **Western flower arrangement is a way of interior decoration, so it's highly decorative, using a lot of flowers of different colors. Meanwhile, ikebana is considered a form of art. Using not only flowers, but also twigs and leaves, ikebana works try to convey the emotions of the creator to the appreciators.**

西洋のフラワーアレンジメントは、室内装飾の手法だから、異なる色彩の花をたくさん使って、とても華美だよね。一方、生け花は、芸術の様式と考えられているんだ。生け花の作品は、花だけでなく、枝や葉も使って、作者の感情を鑑賞者に伝えようとするんだ。

Vocabulary 語句

flower arrangement	フラワーアレンジメント	self-discipline	名 自己鍛錬
originate as ~	~として発祥する	interior decoration	室内装飾
offer A to B	A を B に供える	decorative	形 装飾的な
Buddhist altar	仏壇（**altar** は「祭壇」の意味）	a form of art	芸術の様式
symbolize	動 ~を象徴する	convey A to B	A を B に伝える
harmony	名 調和	emotion	名 感情
as a means of ~	~の手法として（**means** は単複同形の可算名詞で、「手法」の意味）	appreciator	名 鑑賞者

Shodo

書道

What is *shodo*?

Shodo is the traditional Japanese art of calligraphy created with brushes and India ink. The shades of ink and brush strokes are especially important to write beautiful characters. The first *shodo* of the year is called *kakizome*, and people write auspicious words to celebrate the coming of the New Year.

書道って何だろう？

書道は、筆と墨を使って創作される伝統的な日本のカリグラフィです。美しい文字を書くには、墨の濃淡や筆の運びが特に重要です。年の初めに行う書道は書初めと呼ばれ、新年の訪れを祝うために、縁起の良い言葉を書きます。

イラストで くらべる！

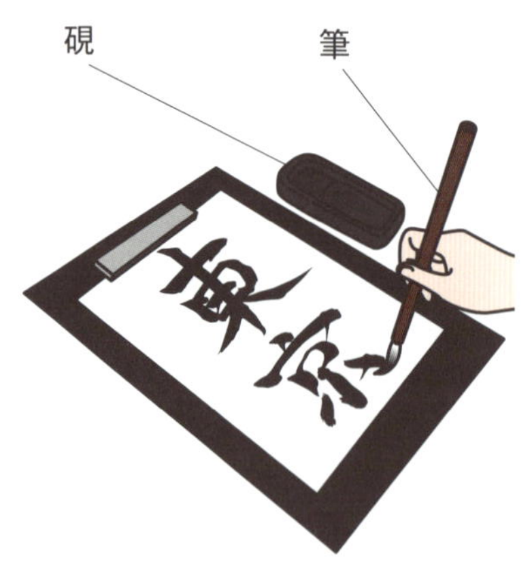

自己鍛錬の方法

文字を美しく見せるための手法

Shodo を英語で説明してみよう

Q. **How is *shodo* different from Western calligraphy?**

書道を西洋のカリグラフィと比べてどう？

A. *Shodo* is regarded as a way to discipline oneself, so it is also practiced as part of school education. In Japan, hand-written words are often thought to represent the personality of the writers, so having good calligraphy skills is important to the Japanese. Therefore, there are many *shodo* schools and correspondence courses.

書道は、自己鍛錬の方法とも考えられていて、そのため学校教育の一部としても稽古されているね。日本では手書きの文字は、書いた人の性格を表すと思われることが多いから、字を書くのが上手なことは日本人にとって大切なんだ。だから、書道の学校や通信講座がたくさんあるんだよ。

🎎 Vocabulary 語句

calligraphy	名 カリグラフィ（筆や特殊なペンなどで美しい文字を手書きすること）
India ink	墨（英国では Indian ink とも）
shade	名 濃淡
stroke	名 ここでは、筆運び
character	名 文字

auspicious	形 縁起の良い
celebrate	動 〜を祝う
discipline oneself	自己鍛錬をする
represent	動 〜を表す
personality	名 性格
correspondence course	通信講座

Kyoten

経典

What is *kyoten*?

Kyoten are Buddhist scriptures that describe the teachings of Buddha. They are written in Chinese, and are usually recited in Chinese as they are by Buddhist monks or followers at rituals such as services for the deceased. Different sects of Buddhism use different *kyoten* in accordance with their doctrines.

経典って何だろう？

経典は、ブッダの教えを記した仏教の聖典です。経典は中国語で書かれており、故人の供養などの儀式において、仏僧や信者が中国語でそのまま朗読するのが普通です。異なる仏教宗派は、その教義にふさわしい、異なる経典を用います。

イラストで くらべる！

中国語　　　　　　　　　　　　　　　　英語

Kyoten を英語で説明してみよう

Q. **Are *kyoten* similar to the Bible?**

経典って聖書に似ている？

A. Yes, they are in that they describe the teachings of the founder. But most *kyoten* were originally written in old Indian languages, and then were translated into Chinese, so most Japanese can't understand them as they are. For ordinary Buddhist followers, *kyoten* are for the purpose of recitation, rather than to be read and understood.

そうだね、開祖の教えを記している点においてはね。でも、ほとんどの経典は古代インド語で書かれて、その後、中国語に翻訳されたものなので、大半の日本人には、そのままでは理解できない代物なんだ。一般の仏教信者にとっては、経典は唱えるのが目的であって、読んで理解するというものではないね。

🌀 Vocabulary 語句

Buddhist	形 仏教の		ritual	名 儀式
scripture	名 聖典、経典		service for the deceased	故人の供養
describe	動 〜を記す		sect	名 （仏教などの）宗
Buddha	名 ブッダ（仏教の開祖の釈迦。大乗仏教では、悟りを開いた如来を意味する）		in accordance with 〜	〜にふさわしい
			doctrine	名 教義
			the Bible	聖書
recite	動 〜を朗読する		be translated into 〜	〜に翻訳される
Buddhist monk	僧侶		recitation	名 朗唱
follower	名 信者			

Zen
禅

What is Zen?

Zen, or Zen Buddhism, was founded in China by an Indian saint named Bodhidharma. It was introduced into Japan in the Middle Ages. Zen Buddhism does not rely on Buddhist scriptures, and emphasizes the importance of the practice of Zen meditation called *zazen*, as a way to attain the state of enlightenment.

訳 禅って何だろう？

禅、あるいは禅宗は、達磨大師という名のインドの聖人によって中国で創始され、中世に日本にもたらされました。禅宗は、仏教経典に頼らず悟りの境地に到達する方法として、坐禅と呼ばれる、禅に基づく瞑想を実践する重要性を強調します。

目的：煩悩を滅すること

目的：健康の促進

Zen を英語で説明してみよう

Q. **How is zazen different from yoga?**

坐禅はヨガとどう違うの？

A. **Zazen developed from yoga, so they are similar. Both are based on the practice of meditation, but their aims are different. The aim of yoga is to synchronize the practitioner's mind and body to promote good health, whereas the aim of zazen is to eliminate worldly desires.**

坐禅はヨガから発達したものだから似ているよ。どちらも瞑想を行うことに根差しているけど、その目的が違うんだ。ヨガの目的は実践者の心身を同期させて、健康を促進することだけど、座禅の目的は煩悩を滅することにあるんだ。

👹 Vocabulary　語句

saint	名 聖人		the state of enlightenment	悟りの境地
rely on ～	～に頼る		synchronize	動 ～を同期させる
scripture	名 教典		eliminate	動 ～を滅する
emphasize	動 ～を強調する		worldly desires	煩悩
meditation	名 瞑想			
attain	動 ～に到達する			

Kendo
剣道

What is kendo?

Kendo is a martial art of Japan. It is a form of swordsmanship fought between two contestants, using a bamboo sword called *shinai* and protective gear including a helmet, a body protector, wrist protectors and a waist protector. Kendo emphasizes the importance of spiritual training and self-discipline.

剣道って何だろう？
剣道は日本の武道の１つです。剣道は、２人の競技者の間で、竹刀と呼ばれる竹製の刀と、面、胴、小手、垂れという防具を使って戦われる剣術の一様式です。剣道は、精神修養と自己鍛錬を重視します。

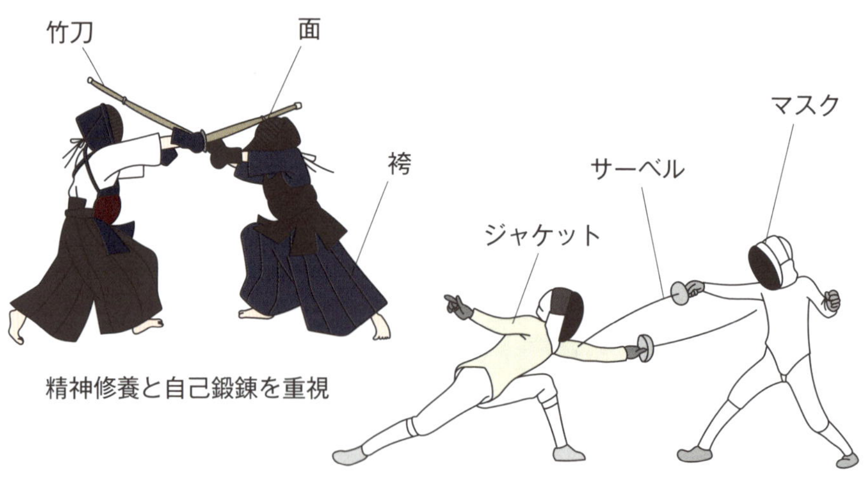

Kendo を英語で説明してみよう

Q. **How is kendo different from fencing?**

剣道はフェンシングとはどう違うの？

A. In fencing, sword skills are the most important in scoring a point, but in kendo, there are three things necessary to score a point. They are called *ki-ken-tai*. *Ki* is to show high spirits, *ken* is to use the sword properly, and *tai* is to maintain the proper posture.

フェンシングでは１本を取るのに、剣の技が一番大切だけど、剣道では１本を取るのに必要なことが３つあるんだ。それらは、気剣体と呼ばれている。気は気合を見せること、剣は竹刀の正しい使い方、そして、体は、正しい姿勢を保つことなんだ。

🔴 Vocabulary 語句

martial art	武道		self-discipline	名 自己鍛錬
swordsmanship	名 剣術		score	動 ～を得る
contestant	名 競技者		point	名 得点、１本
bamboo sword	竹刀		high spirit	気合
protective gear	防具（gear は、「用具一式」の意味）		properly	副 正しく
			proper	形 正しい
spiritual training	精神修養		posture	名 姿勢

Kyudo

弓道

What is kyudo?

Kyudo is a Japanese martial art of archery, whose origins go back to ancient times. After guns were introduced to Japan in the 16th century, archery became a way of spiritual training for samurai. In modern times, it once declined, but later was revived as a way to train the body and mind.

弓道って何だろう？

弓道は、弓矢を使う日本の武道で、その起源は古代にさかのぼります。16世紀に日本に銃が伝わった後は、弓術は武士の精神修養の手段として用いられました。近代になって一時衰退したものの、後に心身を鍛える方法として復活しました。

イラストで くらべる！

Kyudo 弓道 VS Western archery アーチェリー

Kyudo を英語で説明してみよう

Q. **How is kyudo different from Western archery?**

弓道は西洋のアーチェリーとどう違うの？

A. **Western archery uses various bow aids to hit the target easier, but in kyudo, only the bow and arrows are used. Also, in archery, the rating is based only on the scores gained by shooting the target, while in kyudo, not only scores but the form of the shooter is also evaluated.**

西洋のアーチェリーは的を射やすくするために、弓にいろんな補助具を付けるけど、弓道では、弓と矢しか用いないんだ。それにアーチェリーでは的を射ることで得られたスコアのみによって採点されるけど、弓道ではスコアだけでなく、射る人の型も評価されるんだよ。

🟥 Vocabulary 語句

martial art	武道	bow	名 弓（「矢」は arrow と言う）
archery	名 弓術	aid	名 補助具
origin	名 起源	rating	名 採点
go back to ～	～にさかのぼる	gain	動 ～を得る
gun	名 銃	form	名 型
be introduced to ～	～に伝わる	evaluate	動 ～を評価する
decline	動 衰退する		
revive	動 ～を復活させる		

017

Karate

空手

What is karate?

Karate is a Japanese martial art. It developed in the Ryukyu Kingdom, today's Okinawa Prefecture, as a form of unarmed combat in the Middle Ages, and was introduced into mainland Japan in modern times. Karate techniques include arm strikes, thrusts and kicks. Karate will be added to the 2020 Tokyo Olympic Games.

空手って何だろう？ ── 空手は日本の武道の１つです。空手は武器を持たない格闘技として、現在の沖縄県にあたる琉球王国で中世に発達し、近代になって日本の本土にもたらされました。空手の技には打ち、突き、蹴りなどがあります。空手は、2020 年の東京オリンピックにおいて競技に加えられます。

イラストで **くらべる！**

型がとても大切

Karate を英語で説明してみよう

Q. **How is karate different from Thai boxing?**

空手はムエタイとどう違うの？

A. Compared to Thai boxing, the forms, or kata, are very important in karate. Kata are a series of pre-arranged moves performed solo. There are several dozens of kata, and the kata performance is the basic part of karate practice. The kata performance is also a part of karate competitions.

ムエタイと比べると、空手では、型がとても大事だね。型は、1人で演武する一連の決まった動作なんだ。型は数十あって、型の演武は空手の練習の基本的な部分なんだ。型の演武は空手試合の一部でもあるんだよ。

Vocabulary 語句

martial art	武道	be added to ～	～に加えられる
unarmed	形 武器を持たない	Thai boxing	ムエタイ（タイの国技）
combat	名 格闘	pre-arranged	あらかじめ決められた
strike	名 打撃、ここでは、（空手の）打ち技	solo	副 1人で
thrust	名 突き刺すこと、ここでは、（空手の）突き技	competition	名 試合

018

Haiku
俳句

What is haiku?

Haiku is a compact form of Japanese poetry, consisting of three lines in a 5-7-5 syllable pattern. Each haiku poem must contain a season word called *kigo*. Creating haiku requires the use of imagination, so it is popular as a means of education as well as a hobby.

俳句って何だろう？
俳句は、5-7-5 の音節パターンを持つ 3 行からなる、短い日本の詩歌の形式です。それぞれの俳句が季語と呼ばれる季節の語を含む必要があります。俳句を作るには想像力が必要なので、趣味としてだけでなく、教育手段としても人気です。

イラストで くらべる！

Haiku 俳句 VS English poetry 英語の詩歌

音節のパターンが大切

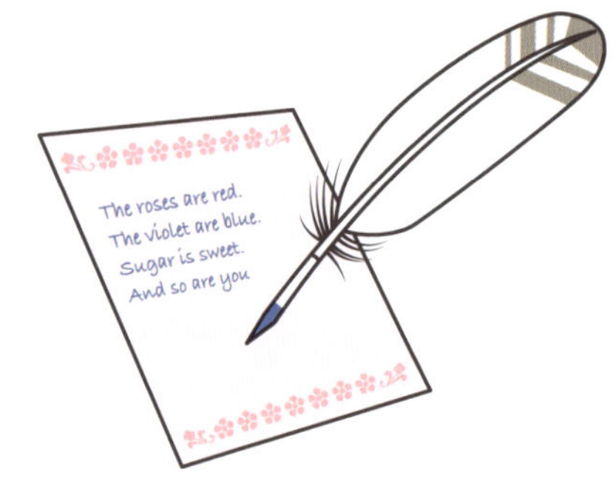

韻を踏むことが大切

Haiku を英語で説明してみよう

Q. **How is Japanese poetry different from English poetry?**

日本語の詩歌と英語の詩歌でどう違う？

A. **Because of the language differences, the basic rules are different. Traditional Japanese poetry such as haiku and *tanka* has fixed syllable patterns, whereas the numbers of syllables vary in English poetry. Also, rhyming is not necessary in Japanese poetry, whereas it is very important in English poetry.**

言語が異なるから、基本的な規則も異なっているね。俳句や短歌などの伝統的な日本の詩歌には、決まった音節のパターンがあるけど、英語の詩歌では、音節の数は様々だよね。それに、日本の詩歌では韻を踏む必要はないけど、英語の詩歌では韻を踏むのがとても大切だよね。

🦗 Vocabulary 語句

compact	形 簡潔な	the use of ～	～を使うこと
poetry	名 詩歌	imagination	名 想像力
syllable	名 音節	as a means of ～	～の方法として
contain	動 ～を含む	rhyming	名 韻を踏むこと
require	動 ～を必要とする		

019

Shogi
将棋

What is *shogi*?

Shogi is a traditional Japanese board game, which is similar to Western chess. The two players place their pieces on the board, and move them in turn. When the king piece of either player is checkmated, the game is over. *Shogi* is very popular in Japan both in amateur and professional circles.

将棋って何だろう？
将棋は日本の伝統的な盤ゲームで、西洋のチェスに似ています。2人の対戦相手が盤の上に駒を置き、交互に動かします。王に相当する駒が詰まれるとゲームは終了します。将棋は日本で、アマ・プロ界ともに人気です。

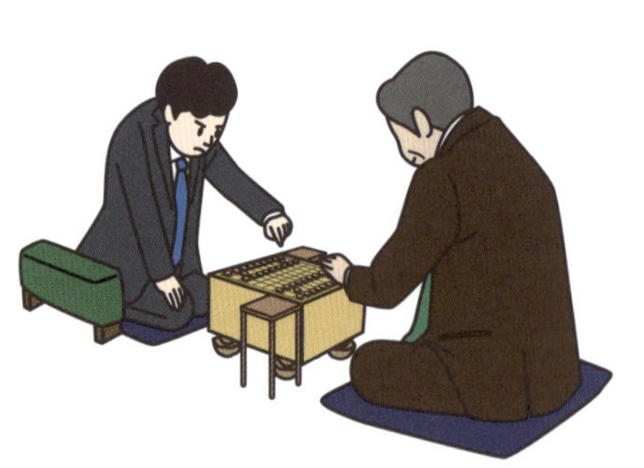

将棋盤（縦横9マスずつ）

チェスボード（縦横8マスずつ）

Shogi を英語で説明してみよう

Q. **How is *shogi* different from chess?**

将棋はチェスとどう違うの？

A. **The rules are a bit different. In *shogi*, captured pieces can be returned to the board by the captor to be used as part of the captor's forces. And, while in chess, only pawns can be promoted, in *shogi*, six kinds of pieces including pawns can be promoted.**

ルールがちょっと違うよ。将棋では、取られた駒は、取った人が自分の戦力として盤面に戻すことができるんだ。それにチェスでは、ポーンのみが成ることができるのに対し、将棋では歩も含めて6種類の駒が成ることができるんだ。

🔴 Vocabulary 語句

board game	盤を使ったゲーム	〜 circle	〜界
similar to 〜	〜に似た	captured piece	取られた駒
chess	名 チェス	captor	名 （駒を）取った人
piece	名 ここでは、駒	force	名 戦力
in turn	交互に、順番に	pawn	名 （チェスの）ポーン（将棋の「歩」に相当）
checkmate	動 〜を詰める（checkmate はチェスの用語で、名詞では自分の王が取られるのを避けられない状態を指す。動詞で使うと、相手の王をその状態に追い込む、つまり将棋でいう、「詰める」という意味になる）	promote	動 （将棋やチェスで）成る（駒が別のより強い駒に変わること）

Karuta

カルタ

020

What is *karuta*?

Karuta is a set of Japanese playing cards. They consist of reading cards bearing a Japanese saying and taking cards bearing the first kana character of the saying and a related picture. In the game, a reader reads out the cards one at a time, and the players compete to pick up the corresponding card.

カルタって何だろう？　カルタは、1組の日本のカード遊具です。日本の諺が書かれた読み札と、その諺の最初の仮名文字と関連する絵が描かれた取り札からなっています。遊戯では読み手が1枚ずつカードを読み上げ、競技者がそれに対応するカードを拾って競います。

イラストで **くらべる!**

Karuta カルタ **VS** Western playing cards トランプ

くらべてスッキリ!

Karuta を英語で説明してみよう

Q. **Did *karuta* originate from Western playing cards?**

カルタって西洋のトランプから生まれたの？

A. **Yes, they did. In fact, its name *karuta* came from the Portuguese word meaning "card". Although the prototype of *karuta* existed even before Europeans first came to Japan in the 16th century, it merged with Western playing cards in the Edo Period and developed into *karuta* as we know it today.**

そうだよ。事実、カルタという名前は、ポルトガル語でcardを意味する語に由来するんだ。カルタの原型は、ヨーロッパ人が初めて日本にやって来た 16 世紀以前に存在していたけれど、それが江戸時代に西洋のカードと融合して、今日、カルタとして知られるものへ発達したんだ。

🔴 Vocabulary 語句

playing cards	カード遊具、トランプ（**trumps** という呼び名もあるが、西洋のトランプは一般に **playing cards** と呼ばれる）
bear	動 ～が描かれている
saying	名 諺
related	形 関連する

read out ～	～を読み上げる
compete to do ～	～して競い合う
corresponding	形 対応する
originate from ～	～から生まれる
prototype	名 原型
merge with ～	～と融合する

021

Kabuki
歌舞伎

What is kabuki?

Kabuki is a form of traditional stage drama. Kabuki is performed only by men, so the female roles are played by male actors called *onnagata*. It is characterized by exaggerated makeup, gorgeous costumes, sophisticated stage sets, and a runway that extends into the audience.

歌舞伎って何だろう？
歌舞伎は伝統的な舞台演劇の１つです。歌舞伎は男優のみが演じるため、女性役も女形と呼ばれる男優が演じます。歌舞伎の特徴は、派手な化粧、豪華な衣装、複雑な舞台装置、観客へ延びる通路です。

大衆演劇

上流階級のための演劇

Kabuki を英語で説明してみよう

Q. **Is kabuki like opera in the West?**

歌舞伎は西洋のオペラに似ている？

A. **Yes, it is in that they both are a combination of drama, music and dance. However, while opera developed as a form of entertainment for high-class people, kabuki developed as popular entertainment. Also, unlike in opera, kabuki musicians and singers often perform on the stage.**

そうだね、どちらも、演劇、音楽、舞踊を組み合わせている点においては似ているね。でも、オペラが上流階級のための演劇として発達したのに対し、歌舞伎は大衆演劇だったんだよ。それに、オペラと違って、歌舞伎の演奏家や歌手たちはステージ上で演じることもよくあるよ。

🟥 Vocabulary 語句

stage drama	舞台演劇	runway	名 通路（ここでは、花道）
perform	動 ～を演じる	extend into ～	～へ延びる
female role	女性の役柄	audience	名 観客
exaggerated makeup	派手な化粧（ここでは、隈取）	combination	名 組み合わせ
gorgeous costume	豪華な衣装	high-class people	上流階級
sophisticated stage set	複雑な舞台装置（ここでは、回り舞台やせり上げなど）	popular entertainment	大衆演劇

Q. **Why do male actors perform female roles in kabuki?**

歌舞伎では、どうして男優が女性の役を演じるの？

A. **Kabuki was begun as a dance performance by a shrine maiden named Izumo-no-Okuni in 1603. Soon, similar performances by prostitutes became popular. The government worried about moral decline, and banned female stage performance. Ever since, it's been a tradition that kabuki is performed only by male actors. The actors who perform female roles are called *onnagata*. Kabuki uses a lot of exaggeration, and *onnagata's* acting style is no exception. They try to exaggerate femininity with skill to look more feminine than real women.**

歌舞伎は、1603 年に出雲阿国という名の巫女によって舞踊の演技として始められたんだ。するとすぐに遊女たちによる似たような興行が人気になってね。政府は道徳の低下を懸念して女性の舞台上演を禁じたんだよ。それ以来、歌舞伎は男優のみで演じるのが伝統なんだ。女性役を演じる俳優は女形と呼ばれる。歌舞伎は、誇張をたくさん使うけど、女形の演じ方も例外ではないんだ。女形は、巧みに女性らしさを誇張して、本物の女性よりも女性っぽく見せようとするんだ。

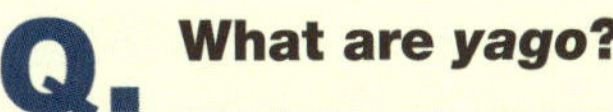

Q. What are *yago*?

屋号って何？

A. *Yago* are kabuki actors' stage family names. They were originally their shop names. In the old days, entertainers belonged to a low social rung, often living on the riverside, but as kabuki actors' influence on society increased, they became able to live on the main street by running a shop there. Today, *yago* are considered a symbol of their status. During kabuki performance, some audiences yell the actor's *yago* at important scenes to boost the excitement.

屋号は、歌舞伎俳優一家の舞台での称号だね。屋号はもともと、彼らが営んでいたお店の名前なんだ。昔は、芸能人は低い社会階層に属していて、河原に住むこともしばしばだったんだけど、歌舞伎役者の社会的影響力が増してくると、表通りにお店を構えることで表通りに住むことができるようになったんだ。今では、屋号は彼らの地位の象徴だと思われているね。歌舞伎の上演中に、大切な場面で雰囲気を盛り上げるために、屋号を叫ぶ観客がいたりするよ。

🎎 Vocabulary　語句

shrine maiden	（神社の）巫女		feminine	形 女性っぽい
prostitute	名 遊女		rung	名 階層
moral decline	道徳の低下		riverside	名 河原
ban	動 ～を禁止する		yell	動 ～を叫ぶ
exaggeration	名 誇張		boost	動 ～を増大させる
no exception	例外ではない		excitement	名 興奮
femininity	名 女性らしさ			

022

Jinja
神社

What are *jinja*?

Jinja are Shinto shrines. They enshrine Shinto deities. Each community has at least one shrine, and various Shinto rituals are held there, such as weddings, festivals, and rituals to pray for the growth of children. During the New Year, big shrines are very crowded with visitors.

神社って何だろう？

神社は神道の神殿です。神社には神道の神が祀られています。各地域に神社が少なくとも１つはあり、そこで、結婚式、祭り、子供の成長を願う儀式など、様々な儀式が行われています。正月には、大きな神社は参詣者でとても混み合います。

イラストで くらべる！

Jinja 神社 **VS** **Western church** 西洋の教会

神道の神を祀る

キリスト教の教会堂

Jinja を英語で説明してみよう

Q. **Are *jinja* similar to Western churches?**

神社は西洋の教会と似ている？

A. Yes, they are. Both *jinja* and churches function as a community center, where community people build their ties. But Shinto has no founder, teachings or scriptures, so at *jinja* people simply pray for their wishes, and the priests help convey their wishes to the deities.

うん、似ているね。神社も教会も地域社会の中心としての役割を果たしていて、そこで地域の人々が絆を築くからね。でも、神道には、教祖も教義も教典もないから、神社では単に願いのために祈り、神職はその願いを神に伝える手助けをするんだ。

🎎 Vocabulary 語句

shrine	名 神殿（神社の訳に用いられることが多い）	function as 〜	〜として機能する
enshrine	動 〜を祀る	tie	名 絆
deity	名 （多神教の）神	founder	名 教祖、開祖
ritual	名 儀式	scripture	名 経典
pray for 〜	〜を願う、〜のために祈る	priest	名 神職
(the) New Year	正月	convey A to B	A を B に伝える

Q. **What are shrine gates for?**

神社の門って何のためのもの？

A. **Shrine gates are called *torii*. They indicate the entrance to sacred space. Many shrines have several *torii* on the approach to the main hall. At *Inari* shrines, where deities of good harvests are enshrined, you may see numerous red *torii* standing close to each other, making a tunnel. They have been dedicated from the followers.**

神社の門は鳥居と呼ばれて、神聖な領域への入口を示すんだ。本堂に至る参道に複数の鳥居がある神社が多いね。豊作の神を祀る稲荷神社では、無数の鳥居がトンネルのようにびっしり並んでるのを見るかもしれないよ。それらの鳥居は信者が奉納したものなんだ。

Q. **How do you pay respect at a shrine?**

神社でのお参りの仕方は？

A. **At the entrance of a shrine, there is usually a water basin. After purifying your hands and mouth there, walk on the approach to the main hall. Throw some coins into the offertory box in front of the hall, and ring the bell by swinging the rope dangling from the bell. Bow twice deeply, clap your hands twice, and pray for your wish. Bow deeply once again before you leave.**

神社の入口には普通、水鉢があるから、そこで手と口を清めた後、参道を歩いて本堂まで行くんだ。本堂の前にある賽銭箱に小銭を投げ入れて、鈴から垂れ下がっている綱を揺らして鈴を鳴らすよ。二度深くお辞儀をして、二度拍手をして、願い事をして、去る前にもう一度深くお辞儀をするんだ。

Q. Why do so many people visit shrines and temples during the New Year?

正月にはどうしてそんなに多くの人が神社やお寺にお参りするの？

A. The Japanese have the idea that bad fortune goes away with the passing year, and everything becomes refreshed with the arrival of the New Year. Therefore, it is particularly important for them to visit shrines and temples at the very beginning of a new year to pray for good fortune to come.

日本人には、旧年とともに悪い運が去って、新しい年の到来とともにすべてが新しく生まれ変わるという発想があるんだ。だから、新しい年の最初に神社やお寺にお参りをして、幸運が訪れるように祈願することが特に大切なんだよ。

Vocabulary 語句

entrance to ～	～への入口		dedicate	動 ～を奉納する
approach	名 ここでは、（社寺の）参道		water basin	水鉢（手水鉢と呼ばれる）
main hall	ここでは、（神社の）本堂		purify	動 ～を清める
deity	名 神		offertory box	賽銭箱
good harvest	豊作		fortune	名 運
numerous	形 無数の		refresh	動 ～を新しくする

023

Matsuri
祭り

What is matsuri?

Matsuri refers to Japanese festivals. Various types of festivals are held across Japan throughout the year. A typical festival is a Shinto ritual of praying to or giving thanks to the deities for a good harvest. It features a parade of portable shrines called *mikoshi* or festival floats called *dashi*.

祭りって何だろう？　祭りは日本のフェスティバルのことです。様々な種類の祭りが全国で1年中行われています。典型的な祭りは、豊作を神に祈ったり、豊作に対して神に感謝したりする神道の儀式で、神輿と呼ばれる移動式の神社や山車と呼ばれる台車が巡行するのが特徴です。

イラストで 

Niinamesai 新嘗祭 VS Thanksgiving Day 感謝祭

天皇が新穀を捧げて、神を祀る

宮中祭祀

七面鳥の丸焼き

家族の行事

Matsuri を英語で説明してみよう

Q. **In America, Thanksgiving Day is a big festival. Do you have a similar celebration?**

アメリカでは、感謝祭が大きな祭りの１つだけど、似たようなお祝いが日本にもある？

A. **Labor Thanksgiving Day might be similar. It is a national holiday observed on November 23 to give thanks for labor and production. But it originated as a court ritual called *Niinamesai*, so unlike Thanksgiving Day, ordinary citizens don't have any special festivities or food to celebrate that day.**

勤労感謝の日が似ているかもしれないね。11月23日に祝われる国民の祝日で、労働と生産に感謝する日だよ。でも、その日は新嘗祭（にいなめさい）と呼ばれる宮中の儀式として発祥したものだから、感謝祭と違って、一般市民がその日を祝うための特別な行事や料理はないんだ。

Vocabulary 語句

typical	形 典型的な
ritual	名 儀式
pray to A for B	A に B を祈る
give thanks to A for B	A に B を感謝する
harvest	名 収穫（物）
feature	動 〜が特徴である
parade	名 巡行、練り歩くこと、行進すること

portable	形 移動式の
float	名 （祭りなどで用いられる）台車、曳山、山車
Thanksgiving Day	感謝祭
Labor Thanksgiving Day	勤労感謝の日
observe	動 （祝日などを）祝う
court ritual	宮廷儀式
festivity	名 お祝いの行事

Q. How are *mikoshi* and *dashi* different?

神輿と山車はどう違うの？

A. *Mikoshi* are portable shrines. In the beginning of a matsuri, *mikoshi* are carried to the local shrine, and the deities enshrined there are moved onto them. At the end of the matsuri, the deities are moved back to the shrine. Because the deities temporarily reside on the *mikoshi,* participants cannot ride on *mikoshi*. *Dashi* are festival floats aimed at leading or accompanying deities, so people ride on them and perform music and dance to attract and entertain them.

神輿は移動式の神社だね。祭りの初めに、神輿は地元の神社へ運ばれて、そこで祀られている神を神輿に移すんだ。祭りの終わりには、神は神社へと戻されるんだよ。神輿には一時的に神が宿っているから、祭りの参加者は神輿に乗っかることはできない。山車はお祭り用の屋台で、神を先導したり神のお供をしたりするためのものだから、人が乗って音楽や踊りを披露して、神を呼び寄せたり楽しませたりするんだ。

Q. Why do people drink sake at matsuri?

祭りでどうしてお酒を飲むの？

A. Some people drink sake during matsuri, but it is proper to drink sake after the matsuri. Rice is sacred food for the Japanese, so sake, made from rice, and rice cakes have been important offerings to Shinto deities since ancient times. Food and drink once offered to the deities are thought to have divine power. In order to receive that power, matsuri participants share them in the ritual called *naorai* after the matsuri.

祭りの最中に酒を飲む人はいるけど、正しくは、酒は祭りの後で飲むものなんだ。米は日本人にとって神聖な食べ物だから、古来、米から作られる酒と餅は、神道の神に対する大切な捧げものだったんだ。神に捧げられた食べ物や飲み物は、神の力を得るとされていて、その力を受け取るために、祭りの参加者たちは、祭りの後、直会と呼ばれる儀式でその食べ物や飲み物を分け合うんだよ。

Vocabulary 語句

portable	形 移動式の		accompany	動 ～のお供をする
enshrine	動 ～を祀る		proper	形 正しい
temporarily	副 一時的に		sacred	形 神聖な
reside on ～	～に宿る		offering	名 捧げもの
lead	動 ～を先導する		divine	形 神の

Judo

柔道

What is judo?

Judo is a Japanese martial art. It is a form of unarmed combat between two contestants. Judo techniques include throwing and pinning. Judo was established by a Japanese educator Kano Jigoro, the founder of Kodokan, in the late 19th century. Judo has been an Olympic sport since the 1964 Tokyo Olympics.

柔道って何だろう？ 　柔道は日本の武道の1つです。2人の選手が武器を持たずに戦います。柔道の技には投げ技と固め技があります。柔道は日本人の教育者で、講道館を創設した嘉納治五郎が、19世紀末に確立しました。柔道は1964年の東京オリンピック以来、オリンピック競技になっています。

イラストでくらべる！

Judo 柔道 VS Western wrestling レスリング

精神修養と自己鍛錬を重視　　　　　力技が主流

Judo を英語で説明してみよう

Q. **How is judo different from Western wrestling?**

柔道はレスリングとどう違うの？

A. **Because judo developed from the traditional Japanese martial art of jujutsu used by samurai, it emphasizes the importance of spiritual training and self-discipline. Although judo is an international sport today, it is still important to show courtesy. In fact, before and after the bout, the contestants bow to each other.**

柔道は、武士が使っていた柔術という日本の伝統武術から発達したので、精神修養や自己鍛錬を重視するんだ。今日では国際スポーツだけれど、今でも礼儀を示すことが大切だね。実際、試合の前と後に、競技者はお互いにお辞儀をするよ。

Vocabulary 語句

throwing	名 投げ技
pinning	名 固め技（pin は、「〜をピンで留める」、転じて「〜を固定する」の意味）
founder	名 創設者
sport	名 競技（オリンピック憲章では、一番大きな枠組みを sport として「競技」、その中に含まれる競技方法が異なる「種別」を discipline とし、discipline の中でメダルを競う各「種目」を event と定義している。例えば、水泳には、飛込、競泳、シンクロナイズドスイミング、水球の 4 つの種別があり、全部で 46 の種目がある。一方、柔道は 1 種別のみで、男女それぞれ体重別に 7 種目あり、全部で 14 種目となっている）
emphasize	動 〜を重視する
spiritual training	精神修養
courtesy	名 礼儀
bout	名 （格闘技などの）試合
bow	動 〜にお辞儀をする

A. **Yes, it does. When male judo became an Olympic sport in 1964 at the time of the Tokyo Olympics, four weight divisions were introduced. Today, there are seven divisions for male and female judo respectively. Still, judo is based on the principle of "softness overcoming hardness", so with proper skill, even a small contestant can throw a big opponent, taking advantage of the opponent's weight and strength. It is another unique aspect of judo.**

うん、あるよ。男子柔道がオリンピック競技になった1964年の東京オリンピックのときに、4階級が導入されたんだ。今では、男子柔道、女子柔道それぞれに7階級あるよ。それでも、柔道は、「柔よく剛を制す」という原理に基づいていて、正しい技能があれば、相手の体重や力を利用して、小さな人でも大きな人を投げることができるんだ。それが柔道のもう1つの独特な一面だね。

Q. Japanese martial arts are called "something-do", such as judo and kendo. What does this "do" mean?

日本の武道は、「○○道」って呼ばれるよね、柔道とか剣道とか。この「道」ってどんな意味？

A. "Do" literally means "the way", and implies the way of self-discipline and good manners. Premodern Japanese martial arts used by samurai were reinvented into modern sports in the late 19th century as a tool of education to train not only physical strength but also mental strength. The word "do" represents such an ideal. Similarly, "do" is used for other forms of art that teach self-discipline and good manners, such as *kado*, flower arrangement, and *chado*, the tea ceremony.

「道」の文字通りの意味は道で、自己鍛錬や礼儀作法の在り方を示すんだ。武士が使っていた近世以前の武術は 19 世紀末に、体力だけでなく精神力も鍛えるための教育手段として、近代的なスポーツに改変されたんだ。「道」という言葉はこの理想を表しているんだ。同じように、生け花を意味する華道や茶の湯を意味する茶道など、自己鍛錬や礼儀作法を教える他の技能の分野でも、「道」が使われているよ。

🟥 Vocabulary 語句

weight division	体重別階級		self-discipline	名 自己鍛錬
respectively	副 それぞれ		good manners	礼儀作法
principle	名 原理		premodern	形 近世以前の
overcome	動 ～に打ち勝つ		reinvent	動 ～を改変する
take advantage of ～	～を利用する		tool	名 道具、手段
imply	動 ～を含意する			

Sumo
相撲

What is sumo?

Sumo is traditional Japanese wrestling and is considered Japan's national sport. It originated as a way to tell fortune in ancient times, and developed into a spectator sport in the Edo Period. Today, professional sumo holds six grand tournaments a year, with each lasting 15 days.

相撲って何だろう？
相撲は伝統的な日本式のレスリングで、日本の国技とされています。相撲は古代に吉凶を占う方法として発祥し、江戸時代には観戦スポーツに発達しました。今日、プロの相撲は、年に 6 回の本場所を開催しており、それぞれ 15 日間続きます。

イラストで **くらべる！**

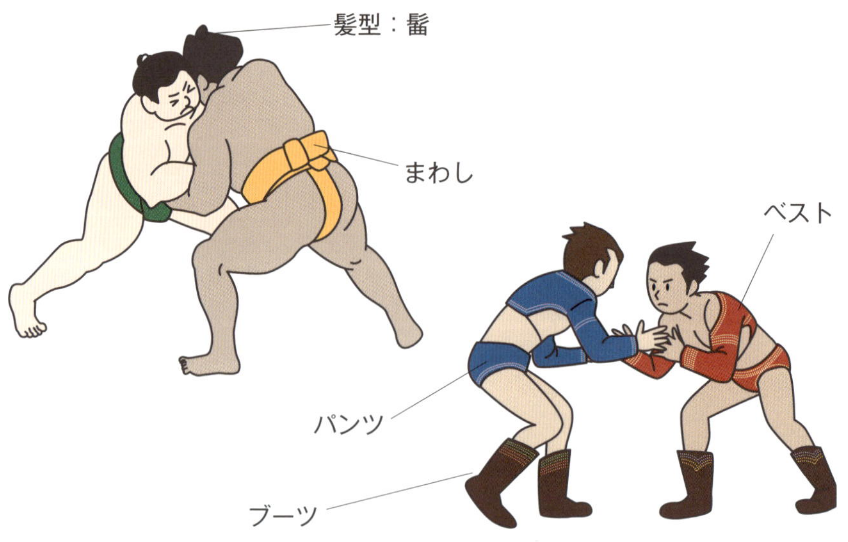

Sumo を英語で説明してみよう

Q. **How is sumo different from Mongolian wrestling?**

相撲はモンゴル相撲とどう違うの？

A. **Sumo developed from Shinto rituals, so it has more ritualistic features than Mongolian wrestling. For example, the wrestlers stomp their feet on the ring. It is a ritual to ward off evil. They also throw salt onto the ring before a bout. It is a ritual to purify the ring.**

相撲は神道の儀式から発達したから、モンゴル相撲に比べると儀式的な特徴が多いね。例えば、力士が四股を踏むけど、あれは邪気を祓うための儀式なんだ。他に、取り組みの前に土俵に塩をまくけど、あれは土俵を清める儀式なんだよ。

🎎 Vocabulary 語句

national sport	国技	**Mongolian wrestling**	モンゴル相撲
originate	動 発祥する	**ritual**	名 儀式
tell fortune	吉凶を占う	**ritualistic**	形 儀式的な
spectator sport	観戦スポーツ	**stomp（= stamp）**	動 （足を）踏み鳴らす、四股を踏む
grand tournament	ここでは、本場所（日本相撲協会が主催する大相撲のうち、番付の昇格を決める公式戦。固有名詞としては、Grand Sumo Tournament と呼ばれる）	**ward off 〜**	〜を祓う
		evil	名 邪気
		purify	動 〜を清める

Q. **How is the winner of a sumo tournament decided?**

本場所の優勝者はどうやって決まるの？

A. During the 15 days of a tournament, wrestlers have one bout a day. The wrestler with most wins at the end becomes the winner of the tournament. When two or more wrestlers are tied for a tournament, playoff matches are held. As a rule, wrestlers from the same stable do not fight each other, but playoffs are an exception. Wrestlers' ranks change according to the results of the tournament.

本場所の 15 日間、力士たちは毎日 1 試合を戦って、最後に勝ち星が一番多い力士が優勝するんだ。2 人以上の力士が同じ勝ち星で場所を終えた場合、優勝決定戦が開かれる。原則として、同じ部屋の力士がお互いに取り組むことはないけど、優勝決定戦は例外なんだ。本場所の成績によって力士の番付が変わるんだよ。

Q. How are sumo wrestlers ranked?

力士はどのようにランク付けされているの？

A. There are six divisions, and the top two divisions called *makuuchi* and *juryo* are a kind of major league and the lower four divisions are a minor league. Wrestlers in the major league are thought to be full-fledged wrestlers called *sekitori*. The highest rank of *makuuchi* is *yokozuna*, a grand champion, followed by *ozeki*, a champion, *sekiwake*, *komusubi*, and *maegashira*. Once the wrestler is promoted to *yokozuna*, he is never demoted, so if he continues to lose matches, he has to retire.

全部で6階級あって、幕内と十両と呼ばれる上位2階級は一種の上位リーグ、下の4階級は下位リーグなんだ。上位リーグの力士は一人前の力士とされ、関取と呼ばれるよ。幕内の最高位は横綱で、大関、関脇、小結、前頭と続くんだ。一旦、横綱に昇格すると降格することはないから、もし負け続けるなら引退しなければならないんだ。

●Vocabulary 語句

bout	名 試合（取組）	full-fledged	形 一人前の
be tied for ～	～に関して引き分けになる	be promoted to ～	～に昇格する
playoff	名 決勝戦	be demoted to ～	～に降格する
stable	名 ここでは、相撲部屋	retire	動 引退する
division	名 階級		

kimono って英語なの？

　英語で日本文化を紹介していて気になるのが、使用する日本語が既に英単語として英語の辞書に載っているかどうかです。英語の文章では、外来語はイタリック体（斜体）を用いるのが普通ですが、英語の語彙に含まれると思われる日本語は普通のローマン体（斜体でないもの）を用いることになります。

　本書では、複数の特定の辞書のうち、どれか１つにでも掲載してあるものは、英語としてローマン体を使い、それらの辞書に見当たらないものはイタリック体にしてあります。今回基準として用いた辞書は、英和辞書が、リーダーズ英和辞典、ジーニアス英和辞典、ランダムハウス英和辞典の３点、英英辞書は、Oxford Dictionary of ENGLISH、THE NEW OXFORD AMERICAN DICTIONARY, Oxford ADVANCED LEARNER'S Dictionary, Longman Dictionary of Contemporary English の４点です。

　kimono はそのいずれにも掲載されていますが、中には、初出年を記録している辞書もあります。ランダムハウス英和辞典によると、kimono の初出は 1886 年ですが、19 世紀末から 20 世紀初頭にかけてヨーロッパで起こった、いわゆる「日本ブーム」（Japonism）の時期になります。ゴッホは、同年、パリの雑誌『パリ・イリュストレ』の表紙で渓斎英泉の浮世絵を見つけ、翌年、それを模倣した『花魁』を描いています。面白いことに、渓斎英泉の絵とは左右反転していますが、『パリ・イリュストレ』に掲載された元の絵自体が左右反転しており、それをそのまま模倣したのでしょう。それに先立ち、クロード・モネは 1876 年に、着物姿の妻のカミーユを描いた『ラ、ジャポネース（日本の女性）』を発表しています。英語に取り込まれた日本語には、その時代の背景が織り込まれています。それを知るのも英語学習の楽しみの１つです。

生活
Life

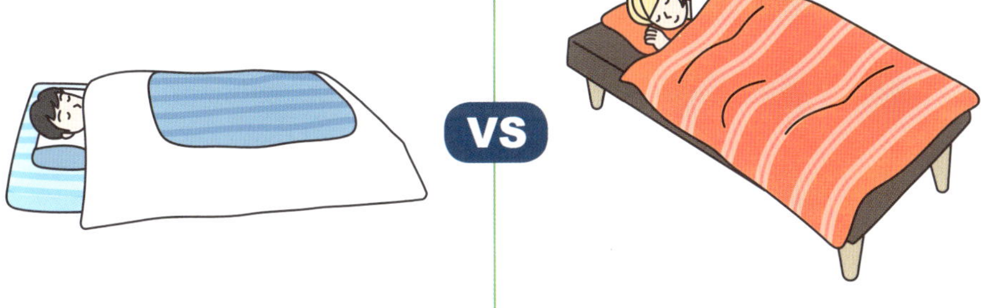

026 Tokonoma
床の間

What is tokonoma?

Tokonoma is a kind of alcove made in a Japanese room. A hanging scroll is usually hung on the back wall, and a vase of flowers is often placed inside. The tokonoma developed in the Middle Ages to add elegance to a rather simple interior of traditional Japanese rooms.

床の間って何だろう？
床の間は、和室に作られたアルコーブの一種です。普通、掛け軸が奥の壁に掛けられ、花瓶に生けた花が内部に置かれることがよくあります。床の間は、かなり簡素な伝統的和室の内装に優美さを加えるために、中世に発達しました。

イラストで くらべる！

Tokonoma を英語で説明してみよう

Q. **In Western homes, beds or a table and chairs are often placed in the alcove. Do you use tokonoma in a similar way, too?**

西洋の家では、アルコーブの中にベッドや、テーブルとチェアを置いたりすることが多いけど、床の間も同じような使い方をするの？

A. **No, we don't. Tokonoma isn't that big. Tokonoma is considered a sacred place, where a deity resides, so it is not a place for people to step on. In a Japanese room, the place closest to the tokonoma is regarded as the head of the table, so guests are usually asked to sit there.**

いや、しないね。床の間はそんなに大きくないしね。床の間は、神が宿る神聖な場所とされているんだ。だから、人がのったりする場所ではないんだ。和室においては、床の間に最も近い場所が上座とされているから、客人はそこに座るように求められるのが普通だよ。

🔴 Vocabulary 語句

alcove	名 アルコーブ（部屋の壁の一部を後退させて作った窪みで、床の間の訳に充てられる）		simple	形 簡素な
			interior	名 内装
hanging scroll	掛け軸		sacred	形 神聖な
vase	名 花瓶		deity	名 神
develop	動 発達する		reside	動 住む、宿る
add A to B	A を B に加える		step on ~	~にのる
rather	副 かなり		the head of the table	上座

73

Fusuma

襖

What are fusuma?

Fusuma are traditional Japanese sliding doors. They are made of a wooden frame covered with Japanese paper. They are mostly used to divide Japanese rooms or as doors for built-in closets called *oshiire*. Various pictures are drawn on the surface, so they also function as interior decoration.

襖って何だろう？

襖は、伝統的な日本の引き戸です。木製の格子に和紙を張り付けて作ってあります。襖は、和室を分割するためや、押し入れの扉に用いられます。表面には様々な絵が描かれており、室内装飾の役割も果たしています。

イラストで くらべる！

Fusuma 襖 VS Western doors 西洋のドア

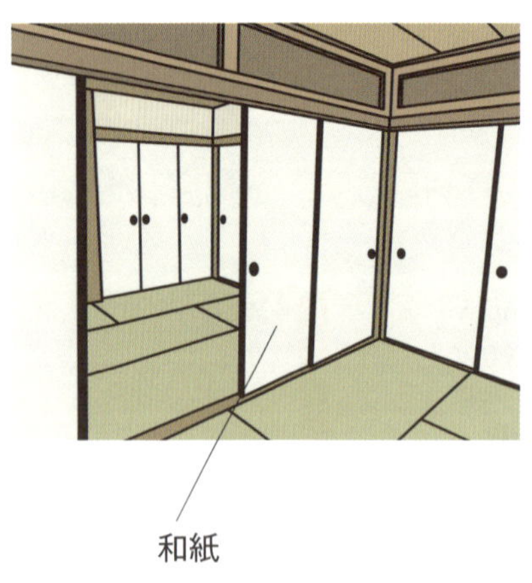

和紙

Fusuma を英語で説明してみよう

Q. Western doors provide better insulation of the rooms. Why do you use fusuma for traditional houses?

西洋のドアのほうが部屋の気密性が高いよね。伝統的な日本家屋では、どうして襖を使うの？

A. Traditional Japanese rooms have standard sizes according to the number of tatami mats placed, so by removing fusuma, you can connect more than two rooms to make a larger space when you have a gathering, for example. With such a design, we can use the rooms for various purposes.

伝統的な和室は、敷かれている畳の数によって大きさが決まっているんだ。だから襖を取り除くことで、集会などを開くときに、2つ以上の部屋をつないで大きなスペースを作ることができるんだよ。そのような設計によって、部屋をいろんな目的で使うことが可能なんだ。

🟥 Vocabulary 語句

sliding door	引き戸		function as 〜	〜として機能する
wooden	形 木製の		interior decoration	室内装飾
frame	名 格子		insulation	名 気密性
Japanese paper	和紙		remove	動 〜を取り除く
divide	動 〜を分割する		connect	動 〜を連結する
built-in	形 作り付けの		gathering	名 集会
surface	名 表面		purpose	名 目的

028 Futon

布団

What is futon?

Futon is traditional Japanese bedding, consisting of a mattress and a quilt. Because futon can be folded up and stored in a closet when not in use, the rooms can be used for different purposes. Also, futon can be hung and dried in the sun, so it's suitable for Japan's humid climate.

訳 布団って何だろう？

布団は、日本の伝統的な寝具で、敷布団と掛布団からなっています。布団は、使わないときには折りたたんで押し入れにしまうことができるので、部屋を異なる目的で使うことができます。また布団は掛けて日干しにすることができるので、湿度の高い日本の気候に合っています。

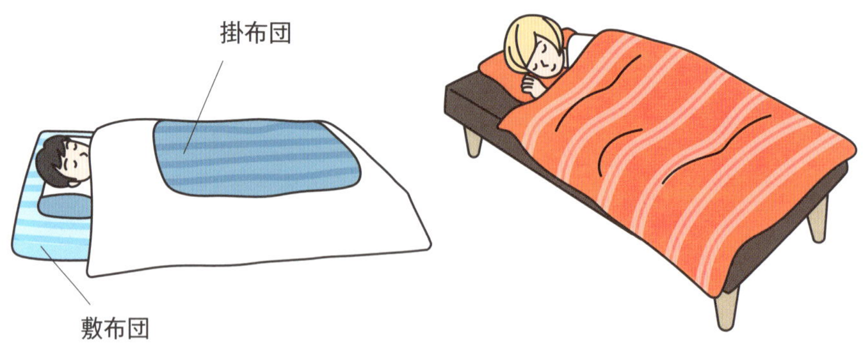

Futon を英語で説明してみよう

Q. **I heard many Japanese use beds today. Is futon still popular?**

多くの日本人が今ではベッドを使ってるって聞いたけど、布団は今でも人気なの？

A. **Yes, it is, although more than half of the Japanese people use beds today according to some recent statistics. Still, futon remains popular especially at traditional places like ryokan and *minshuku*. Also, many homes keep futon sets even today for guests staying overnight.**

うん、人気だよ。ただし、最近の統計によると、半数以上の日本人がベッドを使っているらしいけどね。それでも布団は、旅館や民宿などの伝統的な場所では特に人気を保っているね。それに今でも多くの家庭が泊り客用の布団を持っているよ。

🧧 Vocabulary 語句

bedding	名 寝具		purpose	名 目的
mattress	名 マットレス、ここでは、敷布団		suitable for ～	～に合っている
			humid	形 湿度の高い
quilt	名 キルト、ここでは、掛布団		statistics	名 統計
fold up ～	～を折りたたむ		stay overnight	宿泊する
store	動 ～をしまう			
closet	名 クローゼット、ここでは、押し入れ			

029

Zabuton

座布団

What is zabuton?

Zabuton is a Japanese cushion. It is used when sitting on the tatami-matted floor of a Japanese room. When having a guest, it is customary to offer a zabuton first to show courtesy. In *rakugo*, or traditional comic-storytelling, a *rakugo-ka* performs sitting on a large zabuton placed in the center of the stage.

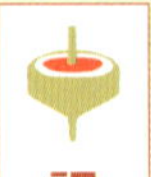

座布団って何だろう？
座布団は、和式のクッションです。和式の部屋で畳の床に座るときに使われます。客人には礼儀作法として座布団を最初に出すのが習慣です。伝統的な滑稽話の落語では、落語家がステージの真ん中に置かれた大きな座布団に座って演じます。

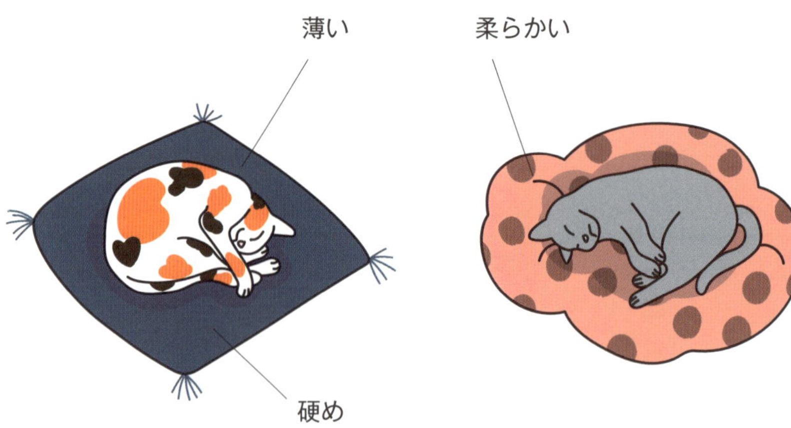

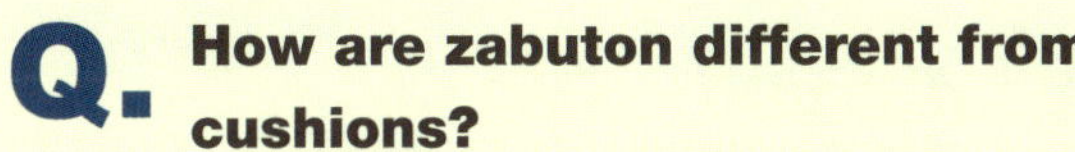

Q. How are zabuton different from cushions?

座布団はクッションとどこが違うの？

A. Because zabuton are designed to sit on, often in the seiza posture, where you sit on your heels, they are made wider, thinner and firmer than usual cushions. Zabuton come in several standard sizes. The common sizes are the size M which measures 55 by 59 centimeters and the size L measuring 59 by 63 centimeters.

座布団は、上に座るためのもので、かかとの上に座る姿勢の正座をすることも多いから、普通のクッションよりも広く、薄く、硬めに作られているね。座布団の大きさは、いくつか決まっているんだ。よくあるサイズは、縦 55 cm、横 59 cm の M サイズと、縦 59 cm、横 63 cm の L サイズだね。

🌀 Vocabulary 語句

tatami-matted floor	畳床	posture	名 姿勢
it is customary to do	～するのが習慣である	heel	名 かかと
courtesy	名 礼儀正しさ	firm	形 硬い
comic	形 滑稽な	come in ～	～がある、～が入手できる
storytelling	名 物語を話すこと		

030

Kotatsu
こたつ

What is kotatsu?

Kotatsu is a traditional Japanese heating device. Kotatsu is a low table with a heater attached underneath. It is covered with a thick quilt, and a tabletop is placed on top of it. There's also a built-in type kotatsu called *horigotatsu*. It has a sunken floor underneath, and users can sit on its edge.

こたつって何だろう？ こたつは、日本の伝統的な暖房器具の１つです。低いテーブルで下にヒーターが取り付けてあります。厚い布団で覆い、上に天板をのせます。作り付け型の掘りごたつと呼ばれるものもあります。掘りごたつは、床が低くしてあり、使う人はその縁に腰掛けることができます。

イラストで くらべる！

Kotatsu こたつ VS Central heating system セントラルヒーティング

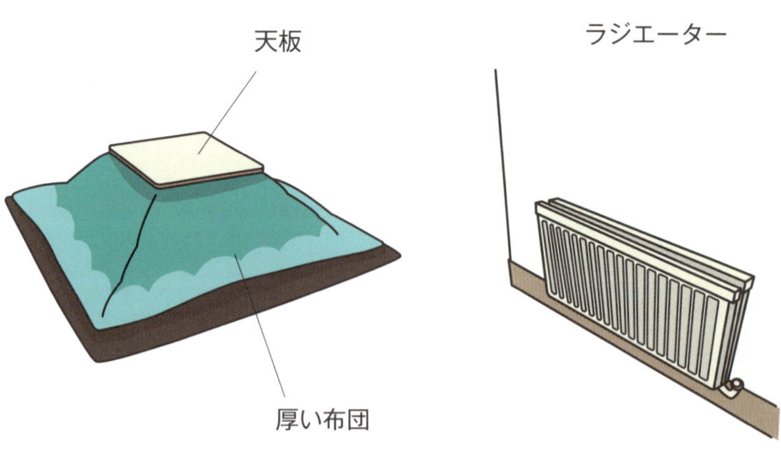

Kotatsu を英語で説明してみよう

Q. **Western homes usually have a central heating system. Is it common in Japan?**

西洋の家では、セントラルヒーティングシステムを備えているのが普通だけど、日本でもよくあるものなの？

A. **In the northern areas, where winter cold is severe, they might have a central heating system, but in other areas, houses are made airy with hot and humid summer in mind, so a central heating system isn't efficient. That's why kotatsu is still popular in the winter time.**

冬の寒さが厳しい北の地域だと、セントラルヒーティングシステムを備えているかもしれないけど、他の地域では蒸し暑い夏を念頭に置いて、風通しが良いように家が設計されているから、セントラルヒーティングシステムはあまり効率的ではないんだ。だから冬の時期には、いまだにこたつが人気なんだよ。

🎎 Vocabulary 語句

heating device	暖房器具	sunken	形 低くした
attached underneath	下に取り付けられた	edge	名 縁
be covered with 〜	〜で覆われる	severe	形 厳しい
quilt	名 布団	airy	形 風通しの良い
tabletop	名 （こたつの）天板	with 〜 in mind	〜を念頭に置いて
on top of 〜	〜の上に	hot and humid	蒸し暑い
built-in	形 〜作り付けの	efficient	形 効率の良い

031

Yukata
浴衣

What is yukata?

Yukata is an informal kimono made of cotton. It is often used as summer wear when people go out for festivals or fireworks displays. Women's yukata often bear colorful summer motifs such as goldfish, morning glories, dragonflies and so on, while men's have more subdued designs.

浴衣って何だろう？

浴衣は、綿でできている略式の着物です。祭りや花火大会などに行くときにしばしば用いる夏の衣類です。女性用の浴衣は金魚、朝顔、トンボなど、色とりどりの夏の意匠が描いてありますが、男性用はもう少し地味な意匠になっています。

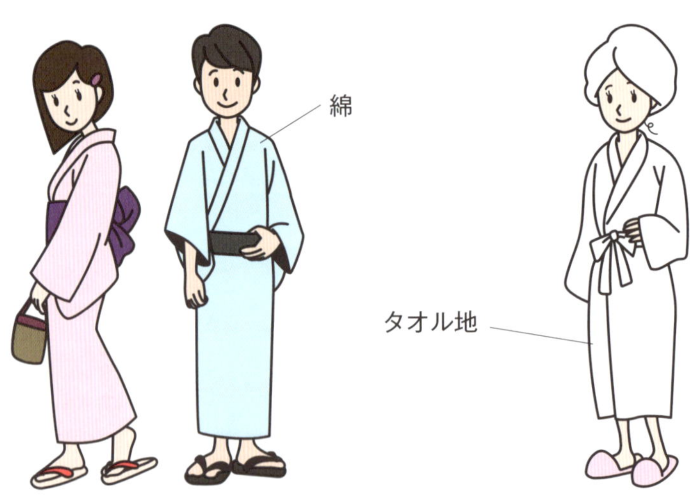

Yukata を英語で説明してみよう

Q. **The book I read says yukata is a kind of bathrobe. Is it correct?**

前に読んだ本では、浴衣はバスローブのようなものって書いてあったけど、本当？

A. **I think the book refers to yukata served at a ryokan. That kind of yukata is used as a bathrobe or nightwear. One difference between a yukata and a bathrobe is that you never go out of your hotel room in a bathrobe, but it is OK to walk around your ryokan in a yukata.**

その本が言及しているのは旅館で出される浴衣だと思うよ。その類の浴衣はバスローブや夜着として使われるんだ。浴衣とバスローブで1点異なるのは、バスローブで自分のホテルの部屋から出たりしないけど、浴衣を着て自分の旅館内を歩き回るのはアリなんだ。

🙂 Vocabulary 語句

informal	形 略式の		goldfish	名 金魚
cotton	名 綿		morning glory	朝顔
summer wear	夏の衣類		dragonfly	名 トンボ
fireworks display	花火大会		subdued	形 控えめの、地味な
bear	動 （意匠などが）描いてある		nightwear	名 夜着
motif	名 意匠、デザイン			

032

Sensu

扇子

What is *sensu*?

Sensu is a Japanese folding fan. It is made of paper pasted on bamboo ribs fixed at the end with a pivot. Various colorful designs are drawn on its surface. *Sensu* is used not only for cooling oneself, but also as an accessory or a prop for stage performances.

扇子って何だろう？

扇子は日本の折りたたみできる扇です。扇子は、端を要で固定した骨に紙を張りつけて作ってあります。その表面には色とりどりの絵柄が描かれています。扇子は、涼を取るだけでなく、装飾品や舞台芸術の小道具としても用いられます。

イラストで  くらべる！

Sensu 扇子 **VS** **Folding fan** ヨーロッパの扇子

Sensu を英語で説明してみよう

Q. I have seen some portraits of European ladies using folding fans. Are they the same as Japanese ones?

ヨーロッパの貴婦人が扇子を使っている肖像画を見たことがあるけど、日本の扇子と同じものなの？

A. *Sensu* were introduced into Europe around the 16th century, and developed in their own way there. They used various materials and ornamental jewelry. Unlike in Japan, however, they were used only as a lady's accessory, and their popularity declined by the early 20th century.

扇子は 16 世紀頃にヨーロッパに伝わり、そこで独自に発達したんだ。ヨーロッパの扇子は、様々な材料や装飾用の宝石を使ったりしているね。でも日本と違って、扇子は貴婦人の装飾品としてしか使われず、20 世紀初期頃には人気が廃れてしまったんだ。

🎎 Vocabulary 語句

folding	形 折りたたみのできる	cool	動 ～を冷やす
fan	名 扇、団扇	accessory	名 装飾品、アクセサリー
paste A on B	A を B に張り付ける	prop	名 小道具
bamboo	名 竹（の）	portrait	名 肖像画
rib	名 （扇の）骨	in one's own way	独自に
fixed at ～	～で固定された	ornamental	形 装飾用の
pivot	名 要（扇の骨を綴じるための釘）	jewelry	名 宝石

033 *Tenugui*
手ぬぐい

What is *tenugui*?

Tenugui is a Japanese hand towel made of cotton. Its origins date back to ancient times, but it became a popular everyday item in the Edo Period, when cotton production greatly increased in Japan. A *tenugui* is rectangular in shape, and usually bears various traditional Japanese designs.

手ぬぐいって何だろう？

手ぬぐいは綿製の和式のハンドタオルです。手ぬぐいの起源は古代にさかのぼりますが、人気の日用品になったのは、日本での綿の生産が大幅に増加した江戸時代でした。手ぬぐいは長方形をしており、様々な伝統的な意匠が描かれています。

Tenugui 手ぬぐい VS Handkerchief ハンカチ

Tenugui を英語で説明してみよう

Q. *Tenugui* is like a Western handkerchief. Is it still popular today?

手ぬぐいって西洋のハンカチみたいだよね。今でもよく使われているの？

A. *Tenugui* have largely been replaced by Western towels and handkerchiefs as an everyday item. Yet, a *tenugui* is still used as a hood or a headband in traditional activities and a stage prop for kabuki and *rakugo*. Nowadays, *tenugui* are regaining popularity as a gift or a souvenir.

日用品としては、手ぬぐいは西洋のタオルやハンカチにほとんど取って代わられてしまったね。でも手ぬぐいは今でも伝統的な活動において頬被りや鉢巻きに使われたり、歌舞伎や落語などの舞台の小道具として使われたりもしているよ。近頃は贈り物やお土産品などとして、手ぬぐいが再び人気になってきているんだ。

Vocabulary 語句

cotton	名 綿		bear	動 （文様や絵などが）描かれている
origin	名 起源		replace	動 ～に取って代わる
date back to ～	～にさかのぼる		hood	名 ここでは、頬被り
ancient times	古代		headband	名 ここでは、鉢巻き
everyday item	日用品		stage prop	舞台の小道具
rectangular	形 長方形の		regain	動 ～を取り戻す

Furoshiki

034

風呂敷

What is *furoshiki*?

Furoshiki is a decorative cloth used to wrap and carry various items. Using various wrapping techniques, you can wrap items of different sizes and shapes, such as long boxes and bottles. *Furoshiki* can be folded compactly when not in use. Unlike plastic bags, *furoshiki* can be used repeatedly, so they are eco-friendly.

風呂敷って何だろう？ 風呂敷は装飾を施した布で、様々な物品を包んで運ぶのに用いられます。いろいろな包み方の技法を用いて、長い箱や瓶など、異なる大きさや形のものを包むことができます。使わないときには小さく折りたためます。ビニール袋と違い、風呂敷は繰り返し使えるので環境に優しいです。

Furoshiki を英語で説明してみよう

Q. **I think bags are the Western counterpart to _furoshiki_. How do you compare them?**

風呂敷に対応する西洋の品というとバッグだと思うけど、比べてみてどう？

A. **Each bag has its own capacity, but a _furoshiki_ can change its capacity depending on how you wrap the item. Japanese like such flexibility. This is true of clothes. Western clothes are designed to fit the wearer, but a kimono can be adjusted to fit any wearer when put on.**

バッグの容量はそれぞれ決まっているけど、風呂敷は物の包み方によって容量を変えることができるよね。日本人はそういった融通性が好きなんだ。これは衣服にも当てはまるよ。西洋の服は、着る人に合うように作ってあるけど、着物は着るときに、どんな人にも合うように調整できるからね。

📛 Vocabulary 語句

decorative	形 装飾を施した	eco-friendly	形 環境に優しい
wrap	動 ～を包む	counterpart to ～	～に対応するもの
item	名 物、品	compare	動 ～を比較する
fold	動 ～を折りたたむ	capacity	名 容量
compactly	副 小さく	flexibility	名 融通性
when not in use	使わないときには（use は名詞）	true of ～	～に当てはまる
		fit	動 ～に合う
plastic bag	ビニール袋	adjust	動 ～を調整する
repeatedly	副 繰り返し	put on ～	（衣類などを）着用する

035

Kamon

家紋

What is *kamon*?

Kamon are Japanese family crests. They are used to indicate the lineage and status of one's family. The culture of using *kamon* first developed among aristocrats and samurai, and then spread among ordinary people. *Kamon* are often printed on a formal kimono, and carved on roof tiles and tombstones.

家紋って何だろう？
家紋は、日本の家系を表す紋章です。家系や家格を示すために用いられます。家紋を用いる文化は最初、貴族や武士の間で広まり、後に庶民にも広まりました。家紋は、正式な着物に付けたり、屋根瓦や墓石などに刻んだりしてあります。

イラストで くらべる！

Kamon 家紋 **VS** **Emblem** ヨーロッパの国のエンブレム

Kamon を英語で説明してみよう

Q. **How are _kamon_ different from emblems in European countries?**

家紋はヨーロッパの国のエンブレムとどう違うの？

A. **Emblems are to identify individuals so they may be different individually even among the same family, while _kamon_ are to identify the family, so it's rare to use a different _kamon_ within the same family. In that sense, _kamon_ are more like the crest in an emblem.**

エンブレムは、個人を見分けるものだから、同じ家系の中でも個人で異なるかもしれないけど、家紋は家系を見分けるためのものだから、同じ家系で異なる家紋を使うのは稀だね。その意味でいうと、家紋はエンブレムの中のクレストの部分に近いね。

Vocabulary 語句

crest	名 かぶと飾り（エンブレムの構成要素の1つで、紋章の兜の上に置かれる意匠。便せんや皿などに家紋として単独で用いられることもある。日本の「家紋」の英訳に用いられる）
indicate	動 〜を示す
lineage	名 家系
status	名 地位、ここでは、家格
aristocrat	名 貴族
ordinary	形 普通の、庶民の
carve	動 〜を刻印する、刻み込む
roof tile	屋根瓦
tombstone	名 墓石
emblem	名 紋章
identify	動 〜を識別する
rare	形 稀な

036

Bonsai

盆栽

What is bonsai?

Bonsai is the Japanese art form of growing miniature potted trees. Some bonsai have been tended for hundreds of years, and are very valuable. They are often displayed on a stand in the garden or on a tokonoma alcove in a Japanese room.

盆栽って何だろう？

盆栽は、小型化した鉢植えの樹木を育てる日本の芸術様式です。盆栽には何百年にもわたって手入れされてきたものもあり、とても価値があります。盆栽は庭に置かれたスタンドに並べたり、和室の床の間に飾ったりします。

イラストで くらべる！

Bonsai 盆栽 VS Potted plants 西洋式の鉢植え植物

植物と鉢が一体となって
自然の美を表現する

草花そのものの
色や形や香りを楽しむ

Bonsai を英語で説明してみよう

Q. How do you compare bonsai with Western-style potted plants?

盆栽と西洋式の鉢植え植物を比べるとどう？

A. The main aim of Western-style potted plants is to enjoy the colors, shapes and fragrances of flowers and plants themselves. In bonsai, however, trees and pots represent the beauty of nature as one, so it's important to keep them in harmony with each other.

西洋式の鉢植え植物の主眼は、草花そのものの色や形や香りなどを楽しむことにあるよね。でも盆栽は、植物と鉢が一体となって自然の美を表現するから、お互いが調和を保つようにすることが大切なんだ。

Vocabulary 語句

miniature	形 小型化した		aim	名 目的
potted tree	鉢植えの樹木		fragrance	名 香り
tend	動 ～の手入れをする		represent	動 ～を表す
valuable	形 価値のある		as one	一体となって
display	動 ～を飾る、～を展示する		keep ~ in harmony with each other	～がお互いに調和を保つようにする
tokonoma alcove	床の間（alcove は、室内や廊下の窪んだ場所）			

Yunomi

湯呑み

037

What is *yunomi*?

Yunomi is a Japanese teacup. It is made of pottery or porcelain, and is used to serve brewed green tea. It has no handle, so people hold it with both hands when drinking tea. For serving *matcha* tea in the tea ceremony, a larger vessel called *chawan*, or tea bowl, is used.

湯呑みって何だろう？
湯呑みは、日本式のティーカップです。湯呑みは陶器か磁器で、緑茶を出すのに用いられます。湯呑みには取っ手がないため、茶を飲むときには両手で持ちます。茶の湯で抹茶を出すときには、茶碗と呼ばれる大きめの器が使われます。

イラストで くらべる！

Yunomi 湯呑み VS Teacup ティーカップ

Yunomi を英語で説明してみよう

Q. **I think it would be easier to use it when it has a handle. Why does it have no handle?**

取っ手が付いていた方が使いやすいんじゃないかな。どうして取っ手がないの？

A. **Western tea is made with very hot water, so a handle is necessary to hold the cup, but because Japanese tea is made with less hot water, we can hold the cup's body directly, and can enjoy feeling the texture of its surface and the warmth of the tea as well.**

西洋のお茶はとても熱いお湯で入れるから、カップを持つのに取っ手が必要なんだけど、日本茶はもっと低い温度のお湯で入れるんだ。だから、湯呑みの本体を直接持つことができるし、同時に湯呑みの表面の手触りやお茶の温かさなども感じて楽しむことができるんだ。

🎎 Vocabulary 語句

teacup	名	ティーカップ、湯呑み	handle	名 取っ手
pottery	名	陶器	the tea ceremony	茶の湯
porcelain	名	磁器	vessel	名 器、容器
serve	動	～を入れる	tea bowl	茶碗
brew	動	（茶やコーヒーなどを）出す（**brew** は「煎じる」の意味で、**brewed tea** は煎茶を指す）	texture	名 手触り
			surface	名 表面
			warmth	名 温かさ

038

Origami
折り紙

What is origami?

Origami is the traditional Japanese art of paper folding, in which a square piece of colored paper is folded into various designs such as cranes, samurai helmets, stars and flowers. Origami originated from the art of wrapping gifts with paper, and later developed into a hobby. Today, origami is popular worldwide.

折り紙って何だろう？
折り紙は、紙を折りたたむ日本の伝統的な技術です。四角い色紙を、鶴、兜、星、花などの様々な形に折りたたみます。折り紙は、贈り物を包む技術から生まれ、後に趣味として発達しました。今日、折り紙は世界中で人気があります。

イラストで **くらべる！**

Origami を英語で説明してみよう

Q. **Is origami similar to papercraft?**

折り紙ってペーパークラフトに似ている？

A. Origami is one genre of papercraft. Papercraft usually refers to card modeling, which uses scale models printed on thick paper. They are cut out, folded and glued together. In traditional origami, however, a single piece of thin paper is folded into a target shape without using glue or scissors.

折り紙は、ペーパークラフトの一様式だね。ペーパークラフトというと普通は、縮小模型が厚手の紙に印刷されている、カードモデルとも呼ばれるものだよ。その模型を切り出して、折って、糊付けするんだ。一方、伝統的な折り紙では、一枚の薄い紙を、糊やハサミを使わずに目標の形へと折って仕上げるんだ。

🟥 Vocabulary 語句

fold	動 ～を折りたたむ		**worldwide**	副 世界中で
square	形 四角い		**papercraft**	名 ペーパークラフト
crane	名 鶴		**genre**	名 様式
samurai helmet	兜		**card modeling**	カードモデル
originate from ～	～から生まれる		**scale model**	縮尺模型
wrap	動 ～を包む		**glue**	動 ～を糊付けする
hobby	名 趣味、娯楽		**target**	形 目標の

039

Shikki

漆器

What is *shikki*?

Shikki is Japanese lacquerware. Lacquerware is made by applying red or black lacquer onto the surface of woodenware as a coating. The lacquered surface is embellished with gold powder, pigments and shell inlay pieces, and finished by polishing it. Popular lacquerware items include soup bowls, layered boxes and chopsticks.

漆器って何だろう？
漆器は、日本の lacquerware です。赤漆や黒漆を、木製の器の表面に塗装膜として塗って作られます。漆面は、金粉や色粉や貝殻の内側の小片などで装飾され、磨いて仕上げられます。人気の漆器には、汁椀、重箱、箸などがあります。

イラストで くらべる！

漆の木の樹液から作られる

油と樹脂から作られる染料

Lacquer を英語で説明してみよう

Q. **Western furniture is often finished with varnish. How is it different from lacquer?**

西洋の家具は、ワニスで仕上げをしてあることが多いけど、ワニスと漆はどう違うの？

A. **Varnish is a coating material made from oil and resin, and lacquer is one type of varnish. Genuine lacquer used for traditional Japanese lacquerware is a thick liquid obtained from the sap of lacquer trees. Because it takes time and effort to collect the sap, genuine lacquer is very expensive.**

ワニスは油と樹脂から作られる塗料のことで、漆はワニスの一種と言えるね。伝統的な日本の漆器に使われる本物の漆は、漆の木の樹液から作られた、ねっとりした液体なんだ。漆を採るのは手間暇がかかるため、本物の漆はとても高価なんだ。

🟥 Vocabulary 語句

lacquerware	名 漆器		shell inlay piece	貝殻の内側の小片
apply A (on)to B	A を B に塗る		polish	動 ～を磨く
lacquer	名 漆		layered box	重箱
woodenware	名 木製の器		varnish	名 ワニス、ニス
coating	名 塗装膜		genuine	形 本物の
embellish A with B	A を B で装飾する		sap	名 樹液
pigment	名 色粉		collect	動 ～を集める

040

Shogatsu

正月

What is Shogatsu?

Shogatsu refers to New Year. On New Year's Eve, the Japanese eat soba noodles, a symbol of longevity, and listen to *joya-no-kane*, the ringing of temple bells nearby. During Shogatsu, people eat special dishes called *osechi*, and visit shrines and temples to pray for happiness. Children receive a money gift called *otoshidama*.

正月って何だろう？ 　正月は、年の初めを祝う期間を指します。日本人は、大晦日に長寿の象徴であるそばを食べ、近くの寺院の除夜の鐘を聞きます。正月には御節と呼ばれる特別料理を食べ、神社や寺院に参詣して幸せを祈ります。子供は、お年玉と呼ばれるお金の贈り物をもらいます。

イラストで **くらべる！**

Joya-no-kane 除夜の鐘　**VS**　**New Year countdown** 新年のカウントダウン

Joya-no-kane を英語で説明してみよう

Q. **Are *joya-no-kane* like the New Year countdown?**

除夜の鐘って、新年のカウントダウンみたいなもの？

A. **These days, more or less, yes. *Joya-no-kane* is originally a Buddhist ritual. Buddhism teaches human beings have 108 worldly desires, so temples ring the bell 108 times to drive them away. Today, however, many places hold special events by combining the *joya-no-kane* ritual and the countdown call to attract more visitors.**

近頃だと、そんなものかな。除夜の鐘はもともと仏教の儀式なんだ。仏教は、人が 108 の煩悩を持っていると教えていて、お寺では、それらを追い払うために 108 回の鐘を鳴らすんだ。でも今日では、多くの地域がもっと参拝客を集めるために、除夜の鐘とカウントダウンのコールを組み合わせた特別イベントを開催しているよ。

🔴 Vocabulary 語句

New Year	正月（年の初めを祝う期間）	money gift	お金の贈り物（ここでは、お年玉）
New Year's Eve	大晦日	more or less	大体
symbol	名 象徴	ritual	名 儀式
longevity	名 長寿	worldly desires	煩悩
peal	名 （鐘の）響き	drive ~ away	~を追い払う
bell	名 鐘（ここでは、お寺の梵鐘）	combine A and B	A と B を組み合わせる
pray for ~	~を祈る		

041

Chugen and Seibo

中元と歳暮

What are *Chugen* and *Seibo*?

Chugen and *seibo* are the seasonal customs of giving gifts to business customers and people who have been helpful. *Chugen* gifts are exchanged in summer, and *seibo* in winter. Popular *chugen* items include beer, chilled sweets, fruits and meat, while popular *seibo* items include sake, wine, ham and ingredients for pot dishes.

中元と歳暮って何だろう？

中元と歳暮は、ビジネス上の顧客やお世話になった人に贈り物をする季節的な習慣です。中元は夏に、歳暮は冬に贈答するものです。人気の中元の品は、ビール、冷菓、果物、肉など、人気の歳暮の品は、酒、ワイン、ハム、鍋物の材料などです。

Chugen and Seibo を英語で説明してみよう

Q. **St. Valentine's Day is a popular opportunity to exchange gifts in many countries. Is it popular in Japan, too?**

バレンタインデーは、多くの国で贈り物を交わす人気のイベントになっているけど、日本でも人気？

A. **Yes, it is, but the way the gifts are given is a bit different. In Japan, it is a day for women to send chocolate to men, often without any romantic feelings. In return, men are expected to give some presents to women on March 14 called White Day.**

うん、人気だよ。でも、贈り物の仕方がちょっと違うけどね。日本では、女性が男性にチョコレートを贈る日なんだ。ただし、恋愛感情は抜きで、という場合が多いけどね。お返しに、ホワイトデーと呼ばれる3月14日に、男性は女性に何かプレゼントをするものと思われているんだ。

🟥 Vocabulary 語句

helpful	形 助けになる		ingredient	名 材料
exchange	動 交換する、ここでは、贈答する（贈ることとお返しすること）		pot dish	鍋料理
item	名 品		romantic feelings	恋愛感情
chilled	形 冷たくした		be expected to do ~	～するものと思われている
sweets	名 お菓子			

042

Nomikai
飲み会

What is *nomikai*?

Nomikai refers to drinking parties usually held at an *izakaya*, a Japanese tavern. It is rare for Japanese workers to exchange frank opinions at their workplace, so they often have a *nomikai* to promote better communication with their colleagues. *Nomikai* is especially popular at yearend and in the early part of the year.

飲み会って何だろう？　飲み会は普通、居酒屋などで開かれるお酒を飲む会のことを指します。日本人の職員が職場で率直な意見を交わすことは稀です。そのため、同僚とのより良いコミュニケーションを促すために、彼らはしばしば飲み会を開きます。飲み会は特に、年末や年始頃に人気です。

Nomikai 飲み会 VS House parties ホームパーティ

居酒屋で

自宅で

Nomikai を英語で説明してみよう

Q. **Americans often have house parties. Is it common in Japan?**

アメリカ人はホームパーティを開くことが多いけど、日本では一般的なの？

A. **Until recently, having a house party was not common in Japan, but today an increasing number of Japanese people enjoy having house parties according to some statistics. Still, in big cities, residences are usually small and there are more drinking places, so many people prefer to have parties elsewhere.**

ホームパーティを開くのは、日本では最近まであまり一般的ではなかったけど、ある統計によると、ホームパーティを開いて楽しむ日本人の数は増えているね。それでも、大都市だと住居は普通小さいし、飲む場所も多いから、どこか他の場所でパーティを開くのを好む人は多いよね。

Vocabulary 語句

tavern	名 居酒屋（地中海地方の飲食店のタベルナを指す英語）	colleague	名 同僚
		yearend	名 年末
rare	形 稀な	statistics	名 統計
exchange	動 ～を交わす	residence	名 住居
frank opinion	率直な意見	prefer to do ～	～することを好む
promote	動 ～を促す		

043

Kingyo

金魚

What is *kingyo*?

Kingyo are called goldfish in English. *Kingyo* are colorful small fish selectively bred in China as ornamental fish. *Kingyo* became a summer symbol in the Edo Period, and a game of *kingyo* scooping became popular among the commoners. *Kingyo* are a popular kimono motif in summer, and also a summer season word in haiku.

金魚って何だろう？　金魚は英語で、goldfish と呼ばれています。きれいな色の小さな魚で、中国で観賞用に選ばれて飼育されたものです。金魚は、江戸時代に夏の象徴となり、金魚すくいが庶民の間で人気になりました。金魚は、夏の着物の意匠で、俳句の夏の季語でもあります。

イラストで **くらべる！**

Kingyo 金魚 **VS** **Tropical fish** 熱帯魚

Kingyo を英語で説明してみよう

Q. **Are *kingyo* often raised as a pet like tropical fish?**

金魚は、熱帯魚みたいにペットとして飼育されているの？

A. **Yes, they are. *Kingyo* are said to live for 10 to 15 years, and many people raise *kingyo* as a pet. However, the species used in the scooping game is rather weak, and difficult to keep alive because they are cultured as fish feed and are shipped while being very young.**

そうだよ。金魚の寿命は、10年から15年だと言われていて、多くの人が金魚をペットとして飼育しているよ。でも、金魚すくいで使われている金魚は結構弱くて、死なないようにするのが難しいんだ。というのは、この類の金魚は飼料用の魚として飼育されていて、とても小さいときに出荷されるからなんだ。

🔴 Vocabulary 語句

goldfish	名 金魚、キンギョ	**the commoners**	庶民（特に身分階級が存在した江戸時代の庶民を指す）
selectively	副 選抜的に	**motif**	名 意匠、デザイン
breed	動 ～を飼育する（英文では過去分詞の **bred** になっている）	**season word**	（俳句の）季語
		species	名 （生物の）種
ornamental	形 観賞用の、装飾用の	**culture**	動 ～を養殖する
symbol	名 象徴	**fish feed**	飼料用の魚
scoop	動 ～をすくう	**ship**	動 ～を出荷する

044 Soryo
僧侶

What is *soryo*?

Soryo refers to Buddhist monks. Buddhism is practiced at Buddhist temples, where Buddhist monks offer services for the deceased and take care of the graves of the families that belong to their temples. To become a Buddhist monk, one has to study Buddhism at temples and academic institutions, and take Buddhist orders.

訳

僧侶って何だろう？
僧侶は、仏教の修行僧のことです。仏教は仏教寺院で行われ、そこでは僧侶が故人のための法要をしたり、そのお寺の檀家の墓を管理したりします。僧侶になるには、お寺や教育機関で仏教について学び、得度をしなければなりません。

イラストで くらべる！

Soryo 僧侶 **VS** Catholic priest カトリックの神父

法衣

仏教の僧

キャソック

Soryo を英語で説明してみよう

Q. **Are *soryo* similar to Catholic priests?**

僧侶って、カトリックの神父さんに似ている？

A. **I think a master of a Buddhist temple called *jushoku* is similar to a Catholic priest. Buddhist monks become a *jushoku* by inheriting his family's temple or by being recommended by the headquarters of their sect. Although Catholic priests remain single for life, Japanese monks including *jushoku* can get married.**

住職と呼ばれる寺院の長なら神父さんに似ていると思うね。僧侶は、その人の家が営むお寺を引き継ぐか、その人が属する宗派の本山から推薦を受けるかで、住職になるんだ。カトリックの神父の場合、生涯独身を保つけど、日本の僧侶は住職を含めて結婚できるんだ。

🎎 Vocabulary 語句

Buddhist	形 仏教の
monk	名 修行僧（キリスト教では修道士を指す）
Buddhism	名 仏教
Buddhist temple	仏教寺院
service	名 （宗教上の）儀式、ここでは、法要
the deceased	故人
take care of ～	～の世話をする
grave	名 墓
belong to ～	～に属する

academic institution	教育機関
take Buddhist orders	得度する（戒を守ることを誓約し、僧名を与えられること）
master	名 長、責任者
inherit	動 ～を引き継ぐ
recommend	動 ～を推薦する
headquarters	名 ここでは、本山（仏教宗派の中の長として末寺を管轄する寺）
sect	名 宗

045

Soshiki

葬式

What is *soshiki*?

Soshiki is a funeral ritual. Most funerals in Japan are based on Buddhism, and are held at a temple or a funeral hall. Mourners hold a wake, and at the funeral on the following day a Buddhist monk recites a sutra in front of the coffin, while attendants burn incense for the deceased.

葬式って何だろう？

葬式は、弔いの儀式のことです。ほとんどの日本の葬式は仏教に基づき、寺院か葬儀場で行われます。会葬者は通夜を開き、翌日の葬式では、僧侶が棺の前で経典を読み上げる間に、参列者が故人に焼香をします。

イラストでくらべる！

Soshiki in Japan 日本の葬式 **VS** Funerals in America 米国の葬式

経典を読み上げる

教会にて

Soshiki を英語で説明してみよう

Q. In America, the deceased are usually buried in the ground. How about in Japan?

アメリカでは、故人は普通土葬にされるけど、日本はどうなの？

A. The deceased are usually cremated at a special facility. After the cremation, the bereaved family and the relatives pick up the bones of the deceased and place them in a jar. Later, another ritual is held to place the jar under the tomb of the deceased.

故人は普通、特別な施設で火葬されるんだ。火葬の後は、遺族や親戚の人たちが故人の骨を拾って壺に入れるんだよ。後日、別の儀式が行われて、その壺を故人のお墓の下に納めるんだ。

🎴 Vocabulary 語句

語句	意味	語句	意味
funeral	形 葬式の、弔いの 名 葬式	sutra	名 教典
ritual	名 儀式	coffin	名 棺
temple	名 寺院	incense	名 香
funeral hall	葬儀場（日本ではセレモニーホールと呼ばれる）	the deceased	故人
		bury	動 ～を埋葬する
mourner	名 会葬者	cremate	動 ～を火葬にする
wake	名 通夜	cremation	名 火葬
Buddhist monk	僧侶	bereaved family	遺族
recite	動 ～を唱える	jar	名 壺、ここでは、骨壺
		tomb	名 墓

046

Tatami

畳

What is tatami?

Tatami are traditional flooring mats used in a Japanese room. They consist of a tightly-woven rice straw base and a woven rush cover. Tatami come in rectangular standard sizes, so the size of a Japanese room is often indicated by the number of tatami mats placed on the floor.

畳って何だろう？

畳は、和室で用いられる伝統的な床材用の敷物です。固く編まれた藁でできた畳床とイグサを編んで作られた畳表からなっています。畳は、長方形で大きさが決まっているため、和室の広さは、床に敷かれた畳の数でしばしば示されます。

イラストでくらべる！

Tatami 畳 VS Carpeted floor カーペット床

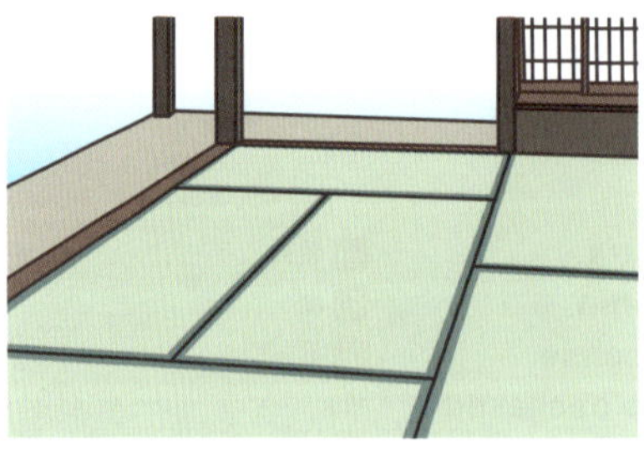

夏涼しい

冬暖かい

Tatami を英語で説明してみよう

Q. **How do you compare a tatami floor with a carpeted floor?**

畳敷きとカーペット床を比べるとどう？

A. **A carpeted floor is warmer in winter, while a tatami floor is cooler in summer. A tatami floor helps adjust the humidity in the room by absorbing moisture, so a tatami floor may be more suitable to the Japanese climate. Unfortunately, there are fewer houses having a tatami room these days.**

カーペット床のほうが冬には温かいけど、畳敷きのほうが夏には涼しいよね。それに、畳は湿気を吸収することで、部屋の湿度を調整する役目を果たしてくれるんだ。ということは、畳敷きのほうが日本の気候には向いているかもしれないね。残念なことに昨今、畳部屋がある家は少なくなっているけれどね。

Vocabulary 語句

flooring	名 床材		standard size	標準の大きさ（大きさが決まっている、ということ）
mat	名 敷物		indicate	動 ～を示す
tightly-woven	形 固く編まれた		carpeted	形 カーペットが敷かれた
rice straw	藁		adjust	動 ～を調整する
base	名 基部（ここでは、畳床を指す）		humidity	名 湿度
rush	名 イグサ		absorb	動 ～を吸収する
come in ～	～のものがある		moisture	名 湿気
rectangular	形 長方形の		be suitable to ～	～に向いている
			unfortunately	副 残念なことに

Q. Why do the Japanese take off their shoes before entering the inside of the house?

日本人は家の内部に入る前にどうして靴を脱ぐの？

A. Japanese residences are traditionally designed for people to sit directly on the floor. Floor cushions, tatami flooring and wooden floored corridors are all designed for that purpose. In order to keep the floor clean, they take off their shoes inside the house. Also, Japanese tend to consider the inside sacred and the outside worldly, and this is true of residences. Taking off shoes at the entrance is a symbolic act of paying respect to the sacred inside area.

日本の住宅は伝統的に、人が床に直接座れるように設計されているんだ。座布団や畳敷きや板張りの廊下も、すべてその目的で設計されている。床をきれいに保つために、日本人は家の内部では靴を脱ぐんだ。また、日本人は、内部を神聖、外部を世俗的と考える傾向があって、これは住宅にも当てはまるんだ。入口で靴を脱ぐのは、神聖な内部空間に対して敬意を払う象徴的な行いと言えるね。

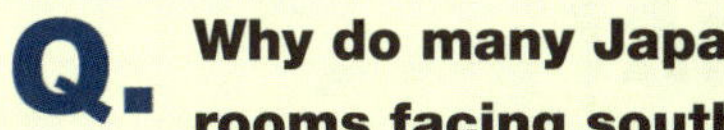

Q. Why do many Japanese prefer rooms facing south?

日本人はどうして南向きの部屋を好むの？

A. Japanese houses are designed to have good ventilation with hot and humid summers in mind. Such a design is not suitable for central heating, and the rooms facing north get extremely cold during winter. The rooms facing south let in a lot of sunlight during winter, which keeps them warm, while they let in less direct sunlight during summer due to Japan's latitude, which is lower than that of most European countries. Thus, the rooms facing south are very comfortable throughout the year.

日本の家は、暑くて湿度が高い夏を念頭に置いて、通気が良いように設計されているんだ。そのような設計だと、セントラルヒーティングには向いていないから、冬には北向きの部屋がとても寒くなるんだ。南向きの部屋は、冬にたっぷり日差しが入って暖かい一方で、ヨーロッパのほとんどの国よりも日本は低い緯度に位置しているから、夏にはそれほど直射日光が入ってこないんだ。つまり、南向きの部屋は、1年を通じてとても快適だということだね。

Vocabulary 語句

residence	名 住宅	pay respect to ～	～に敬意を払う
corridor	名 廊下	ventilation	名 通気
sacred	形 神聖な	humid	形 湿度が高い
worldly	形 世俗的な	suitable for ～	～に向いている
be true of ～	～に当てはまる	latitude	名 緯度
symbolic	形 象徴的な		

047

Tojiki
陶磁器

What is *tojiki*?

Tojiki refers to both *toki*, or pottery, and *jiki*, or porcelain. Pottery making started in Japan in the 8th century, when the use of glaze was introduced. Meanwhile, porcelain production in Japan was started by a Korean potter in the early 17th century in Arita in today's Saga Prefecture.

陶磁器って何だろう？
陶磁器は、陶器と磁器の両方を指します。陶器の製造は、日本では、釉薬が伝えられた 8 世紀に始まりました。一方、磁器の製造は、17 世紀初期に朝鮮の陶工によって現在の佐賀県の有田で始められました。

Japanese porcelain 日本の磁器　**VS**　**European porcelain** ヨーロッパの磁器

Jiki を英語で説明してみよう

Q. **How is Japanese porcelain different from European porcelain?**

日本の磁器は、ヨーロッパの磁器とどう違うの？

A. **European porcelain developed in Germany, copying after pieces produced in China and Japan. In the process of finding the proper material, they tried adding bone powder to the clay. Even after finding kaolin, the real porcelain material, they continued to add bone powder. That's why European porcelain is called bone china.**

ヨーロッパの磁器は、日本産や中国産の磁器を模倣しながらドイツで発達したんだ。正しい材料を探す中で、試しに骨の粉を粘土に加えたんだよ。磁器の本当の材料であるカオリンが見つかった後も、骨の粉を入れ続けたんだ。だから、ヨーロッパの磁器はボーンチャイナと呼ばれるんだ。

🎎 Vocabulary　語句

pottery	名 陶器	proper	形 正しい
porcelain	名 磁器	bone powder	骨の粉
glaze	名 釉薬、釉（ゆうやく・うわぐすり）（陶器や磁器の表面を覆うガラス質）	kaolin	名 カオリン（磁器の材料となる白磁石）
introduce	動 ～をもたらす	bone china	ボーンチャイナ（ヨーロッパで製造される、骨の粉を含む薄い磁器）
potter	名 陶工		
copy after ～	～を模倣する		

Q. **What is the difference between pottery and porcelain?**

陶器と磁器はどこが違うの？

A. The basic difference is the materials. Pottery uses fine clay, while porcelain uses porcelain stone known as kaolin. The firing temperatures for porcelain are usually higher than those for pottery. As a result of these differences, porcelain looks a bit translucent, and has hard and smooth textures, while pottery looks opaque, and has a coarse texture.

基本的な違いは材料。陶器はきめの細かい土を使うけど、磁器はカオリンと呼ばれる陶石を粉にしたものを使うんだ。焼成温度は、普通、磁器のほうが陶器より高い。こういった違いから、磁器はやや半透明で、手触りが堅くて滑らかなのに対し、陶器は不透明で手触りがザラザラしてるよ。

Q. **How are pottery and porcelain made?**

陶器や磁器はどうやって作られるの？

A. Their manufacturing processes are basically the same. First, the materials are mixed with water and kneaded into desired shapes often using a wheel. They are fired and then underglaze paintings are made on the surface. After being glazed, they are baked again to finish. If necessary, overglaze paintings may be made and fired again to stabilize the pigment.

作り方は基本的に同じ。最初に原料を水と混ぜて、こねて好みの形にする。ろくろを使うことが多いね。それを焼いて、表面に下絵付けをするんだ。釉薬をかけた後、再度、焼き上げて完成。必要であれば、上絵付をして、顔料を定着させるためにもう一度焼くこともあるね。

Q. What are some of the ceramics unique to Japan?

日本独特の焼物にどんなのがある？

A. I think Raku ware is unique. Raku pieces are formed by hand without using a wheel, so they are a little deformed and look asymmetrical. Because of their natural shapes, Raku tea bowls better fit the palm when held. Another unique brand is Oribe, which was produced in the early 17th century. Oribe pieces are characterized by their distorted shapes and distinctive greenish color.

楽焼が独特だと思うね。楽焼は、ろくろを使わずに、手で形成されるから、少し変形していて、左右非対称に見えるんだ。その自然な形のおかげで、楽焼の茶碗は持ったときに手のひらによくフィットするんだよ。もう1つ独特なブランドに織部があるね。織部は17世紀初期に作られたんだ。織部焼はその歪んだ形と独特の緑っぽい色が特色だね。

🎎 Vocabulary 語句

translucent	形 半透明の		overglaze painting	上絵（釉薬の上に描く文様）
opaque	形 不透明の		stabilize	動 ～を定着させる
knead	動 （粘土などを）こねる		pigment	名 顔料
wheel	名 ろくろ		deformed	形 変形した
underglaze painting	下絵（釉薬の下に描く文様）		palm	名 手のひら
			greenish	形 緑っぽい

048

Kana

仮名

What is kana?

Kana are phonetic characters used in the Japanese writing system. They were made from simplified kanji, or Chinese characters, which are ideograms. There are two types: hiragana and katakana. Hiragana are mainly used to supplement kanji, and katakana are mainly used to write loan words.

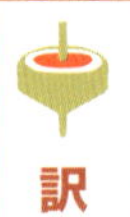

仮名って何だろう？　仮名は、日本語の表記体系において用いられる表音文字です。仮名は、簡略化した漢字から作られました。漢字は表意文字です。仮名には、ひらがなとカタカナの２種類があります。ひらがなは、主に漢字を補完するために用いられ、カタカナは主に外来語の表記に用いられます。

イラストでくらべる！

Kana 仮名 **VS** Alphabet アルファベット

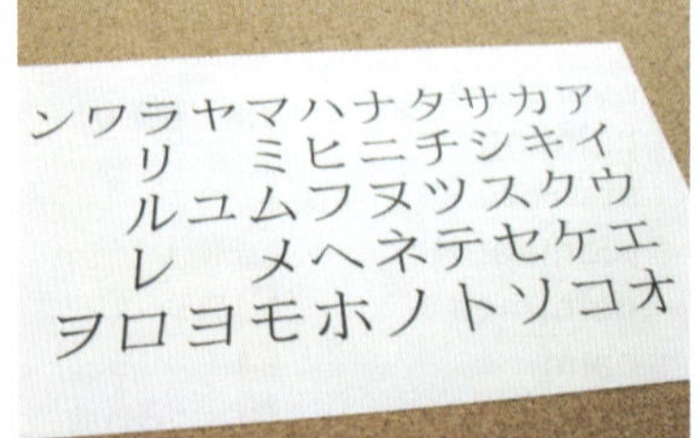

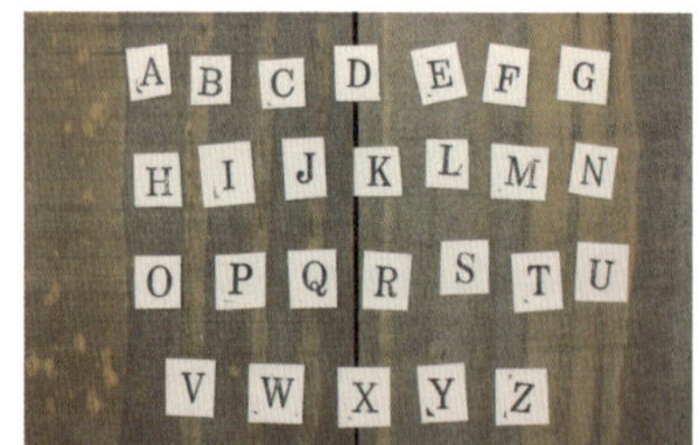

Kana を英語で説明してみよう

Q. **Kana are similar to an alphabet, aren't they? Can you write Japanese in an alphabet, too?**

仮名ってアルファベットに似ているよね？日本語をアルファベットで書くこともできる？

A. **They are similar, but unlike alphabet letters, each kana represents a specific syllable in the Japanese language. Japanese syllables are simple, each consisting of either a vowel alone or a consonant plus a vowel. As Japanese has fewer vowels and consonants, it's easy to write it in the Roman alphabet, too.**

似ているね。だけどアルファベットの文字と違って、1つ1つの仮名は日本語における特定の音節を表すんだ。日本語の音節は単純で、どれも、母音だけか、あるいは、子音プラス母音でできている。日本語は母音も子音も少ないから、ローマ字のアルファベットで表記するのは簡単だよ。

🎎 Vocabulary 語句

phonetic character	表音文字（音を表す文字）	loan word	外来語
writing system	表記体系	represent	動 ～を表す
simplified	形 簡略化された	specific	形 特定の
ideogram	名 表意文字（特定の意味を表す文字）	syllable	名 音節
		vowel	名 母音
supplement	動 ～を補完する	consonant	名 子音

Q. **Why do the Japanese use several different sets of characters in writing?**

どうして日本人は複数の異なる文字を使って日本語を書くの？

A. **In the old days, the Japanese used Chinese for writing, and often read it based on the Japanese grammatical order while pronouncing kanji Chinese characters in either the Chinese or the Japanese ways depending on the context. Around the 10th century, they invented phonetic characters called kana to describe their own spoken language. Still, they kept using kanji characters for conceptual words and set phrases. The result is a mix of kanji and kana characters.**

昔、日本人は日本語を書くのに中国語を使っていて、それを日本語文法の順番で読んで、文脈によって、漢字を中国式（音読）か日本式（訓読）で読んでいたんだ。10 世紀頃に、日本人は自分たちの話し言葉を表すための仮名と呼ばれる表音文字を発明したんだ。それでも、概念を示す言葉や成句には漢字を使い続けたんだ。その結果が、漢字と仮名を混ぜたものなんだよ。

A. Hiragana and katakana have 46 characters each. School children learn how to read and write them in the first grade at elementary school. Although there are said to be about 50,000 kanji used in Japan including names of people and places, the number of kanji designated for everyday use is 2,136 as of 2018. Japanese children have to learn about 1,000 kanji before graduating elementary school and the rest before graduating junior high school.

平仮名と片仮名は 46 文字ずつだね。学童は、小学校 1 年生のときに、それらの読み書きを習うんだ。日本で使われている漢字は、人名・地名を含めて 5 万字ほどと言われているけど、2018 年の時点で常用漢字に指定されているのは 2,136 字だね。日本の子供は小学校を卒業するまでにおよそ 1,000 字、残りは中学校を卒業するまでに学ばなくてはならないんだ。

🎎 Vocabulary 語句

grammatical	形 文法的な	describe	動 ～を表す
context	名 文脈	conceptual	形 概念の
invent	動 ～を発明する	designate	動 ～を指定する

049

Kyureki

旧暦

What is *kyureki*?

Kyureki is the old calendar, which was used until the mid 19th century in Japan. The year length was based on the Earth's revolution around the sun, and the month length on the wax and wane of the moon. Many of Japan's traditional events are still based on the dates of the old calendar.

旧暦って何だろう？

旧暦は、昔の暦で、日本では 19 世紀半ばまで使われていました。1 年の長さは、地球の公転時間に基づいており、ひと月の長さは、月の満ち欠けに基づいていました。日本の伝統行事の多くは、今でも、旧暦の日付に基づいています。

Kyureki 旧暦 VS Gregorian calendar グレゴリオ暦

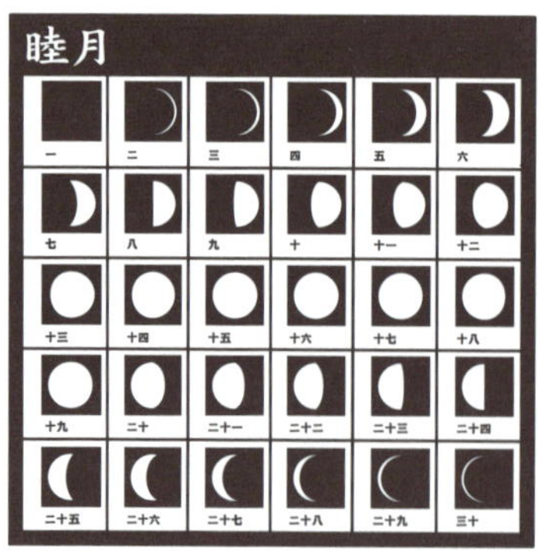

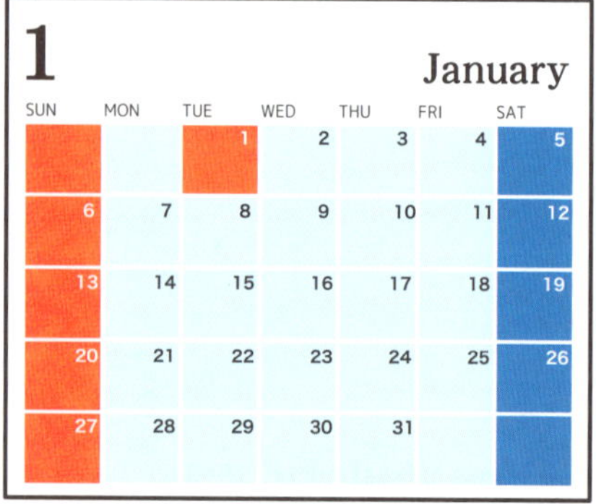

Kyureki を英語で説明してみよう

Q. **Is the old calendar still used along with the Gregorian calendar?**

今でも旧暦はグレゴリオ暦と並んで用いられているの？

A. **Yes, it is. Many Japanese calendars also show the old calendar dates, which have about a one-month difference with the Gregorian calendar. Many aspects of Japanese culture are based on the old calendar, such as season words used in haiku poetry, so it's convenient to know the old calendar dates as well.**

うん、そうだよ。多くの日本のカレンダーは旧暦の日付ものせているんだ。旧暦の日付は、グレゴリオ暦との間におよそひと月のずれがあるね。俳句の季語のように、日本文化の多くの側面が今でも旧暦に基づいているんだ。だから、旧暦の日付を知っておくのは便利なわけ。

🔴 Vocabulary 語句

the old calendar	旧暦（正確には、「太陰太陽暦」lunisolar calendar と呼ばれる）	the wax and wane of the moon	月の満ち欠け
length	名 長さ	traditional event	伝統行事
be based on ～	～に基づく	the Gregorian calendar	グレゴリオ暦（1873 年から日本で使われている暦）
the Earth's revolution around the sun	公転（the Earth's revolution だけでも意味は通じる）	aspect	名 側面
		convenient	形 便利

Many Asian countries celebrate the New Year based on the old calendar. How about Japan?

アジアの多くの国は、新年を旧暦で祝うけど、日本ではどうなの？

A. **Japan celebrates the New Year based on the Gregorian calendar, but the influence of the old calendar remains. The old New Year comes around late January to mid-February on the new calendar, so for the Japanese, the New Year signifies the start of spring. That's why the plum blossoms, which bloom in February, are often used as a symbol of the New Year, and we often write on our New Year greeting cards such celebratory words as *shinshun* meaning "new spring", or *gashun* meaning "happy spring".**

日本では、新年はグレゴリオ暦で祝うんだけど、旧暦の影響は残っているよ。旧正月は、新暦の1月下旬から2月中旬頃にやってくるから、日本人にとって、正月は春を意味するものなんだ。だから、2月に開花する梅の花が新年の象徴に用いられたり、年賀状に、「新春」や「賀春」といったお祝いの言葉を書いたりすることが多いんだよ。

Q. **Do you think the old calendar was useful for people in the old days?**

旧暦は昔の人にとって、有用だったと思う？

A. **I think it was when the moonlight was the only illumination at night. In the old calendar, the first day of each month is the new moon day, and the 15th is the full moon day. So, people could know the date of the month from the shape of the moon, and important nighttime events such as O-Bon, a Buddhist ceremony to console the spirits of the deceased, were held around the 15th under the full moon.**

夜の照明が月明かりだけだった時代はそうだったと思うよ。旧暦では月の最初の日が新月の日で、15 日が満月の日なんだ。だから、月毎の日付を月の形から知ることができたし、故人の魂を慰める仏教儀式のお盆のような夜の大切なイベントは、15 日を中心に満月の下で行われたんだ。

Vocabulary 語句

signify	動 ～を意味する	the new moon	新月
celebratory	形 お祝いの	the full moon	満月
useful	形 有用な	console	動 ～を慰める
illumination	名 照明	the deceased	故人

050

Miai

見合い

What is miai?

Miai is an arranged meeting of a man and a woman interested in marriage. A miai is arranged by a go-between called *nakodo*. After the miai, the pair decides on their own whether to continue to meet. Because it is difficult to find a go-between these days, some people use paid miai services.

見合いって何だろう？　見合いは、結婚に興味がある男性と女性の取り決められた会合です。見合いは、仲人と呼ばれる仲介者が手配します。見合いの後、両者は自らの意思で会い続けるかどうかを決めます。近頃は、仲人を見つけるのが難しいため、有料の見合いサービスを使う人もいます。

イラストで くらべる！

Miai 見合い **VS** Arranged marriage 親が決める結婚

親が結婚相手を決める

Miai を英語で説明してみよう

Q. In some Asian countries, parents choose spouses for their children. Is it common in Japan, too?

アジアの国では、親が子供の結婚相手を決めることがあるけど、それって日本でもよくあることなの？

A. No, it isn't. Until the end of World War II, such an arranged marriage was quite common in Japan, too. However, the new Japanese constitution after World War II guarantees freedom of marriage, and most Japanese today get married of their own free will, regardless of their parents' opinions.

いいや、ないね。そのような決められた結婚は、第二次世界大戦が終わるまでは日本でもよく見られたけどね。戦後の新しい日本国憲法は、結婚の自由を保証していて、今の日本人のほとんどは親の意見とは関係なく、自分の自由な意思で結婚しているよ。

🇩 Vocabulary 語句

arranged	形 取り決められた	spouse	名 配偶者
arrange	動 ～を手配する	constitution	名 憲法
go-between	名 仲人、仲介者	guarantee	動 ～を保証する
decide whether to do ～	～するかどうかを決める	freedom of marriage	結婚の自由
on one's own	自分で	free will	自由意志
paid miai services	ここでは、有料の結婚相談サービス	regardless of ～	～とは関係なく

Q. **What are traditional Japanese weddings like?**

伝統的な日本の結婚式ってどんな感じ？

A. **Traditional wedding ceremonies are conducted according to Shinto rites. The bride and bridegroom are dressed in traditional kimono, and in front of a kamidana, a built-in shrine at the wedding hall, they exchange ceremonial sake and swear an oath of loyalty to each other. After the ceremony, they usually hold a banquet in another hall where food and drink are served for the guests. It is customary for the couple to change their costumes from traditional to Western in the middle of the banquet.**

伝統的な結婚式は神道の儀式に則って行われるよ。新郎新婦は伝統的な着物を着て、結婚式場に備え付けの神棚の前で、酒を酌み交わす儀式を行い、お互いに忠誠を誓う。式が終わると、別の会場で宴会を開くのが普通で、来賓に酒食を提供するんだ。新郎新婦は、宴会の途中で、伝統的な衣装から、西洋的な衣装へと着替えるのが習慣だね。

Q. **Why do you give money gifts to marring couples?**

どうして結婚するカップルにお金の贈り物をするの？

A. **In Japan, money is thought to be a formal gift at important occasions, as long as it is presented properly in a special envelope. And, weddings are one such occasion. Weddings in Japan are very costly because it is often thought to be the union of not only the couple themselves but of their families as well. The procedures to deepen the relationships between the two families and entertain the guests are elaborate, with a ritual, a banquet and mementos for the guests. In order to lessen the financial burden of the couple, it is a custom for the guests to offer them a gift of money.**

日本では、お金は大切な行事での正式な贈り物とされているんだ、専用の封筒に入れて正しい贈り方をする限りにおいてはね。で、結婚式はそのような行事の１つなわけ。日本での結婚式は、新郎新婦だけでなく、彼らの家族もまた結びつく儀式だと思われていることが多いから、とても高くつくんだ。両家の親睦を深めたり、来賓をもてなしたりするための手順が、儀式から宴会から引き出物と、とても凝っているんだ。新郎新婦の経済的負担を軽くするために、来賓はお金の贈り物をするのが習慣なんだよ。

🎎 Vocabulary 語句

conduct	動 ～を執り行う		properly	副 正しく
bride	名 新婦		envelope	名 封筒
bridegroom	名 新郎		costly	形 高くつく
exchange	動 ～を交わす		elaborate	形 凝った
swear an oath	誓いを述べる		memento	名 思い出の品、ここでは、引き出物
banquet	名 宴会			
occasion	名 （重要な）行事		financial burden	経済的負担

kimono って可算名詞？

　英語には集合名詞という概念があります。clothing（衣類）や furniture（家具）などがその例で、これらは不可算名詞になりますが、それぞれのジャンルの中で、形状・用途が共通するものは可算名詞になります。例えば、clothing の中で形状・用途が同じ、jacket（上着）、shirt（シャツ）、trousers（ズボン、足を通す部分が左右に分かれているため常に複数）は数えることができます。同じように、furniture の中でも、chair（椅子）、table（卓）、sofa（ソファ）などは数えられます。

　さて、日本語の「着物」は、衣服の総称（この場合、clothing の意味）、あるいは、着物の上着（この場合、英語の robe に近い）の意味で用いられ、前者では不可算名詞、後者では可算名詞の感覚になります。しかし、どの辞書も、kimono は可算名詞としており、複数形は kimonos になっています。これは、ゴッホの『花魁』や、モネの『ラ、ジャポネース』を見て分かるように、それぞれに描かれているのは打掛で、着物が英語の語彙に加わった当時、着物は、robe のようなものを指す語と考えられたからでしょう。

　しかし、英語を書いていると、着物が clothing の意味である場合もありますし、複数の着物に対し、kimonos と〜 s を付けると、他の日本語との一貫性が乱れるため、やや抵抗もあります。そこで本書では、日本語に関して、可算・不可算かは文脈によって使い分け、かつ、可算名詞の概念の場合、単数形では冠詞を打ちますが（例えば、A kimono is 〜 .）、複数形では、〜 s を付けずに単複同形の語として表記してあります（例えば、Kimono are 〜 .）。日本語の英語表記に決まったルールはないのですが、英語を書く側において一貫性を保つことが大切だと思います。

食べ物・飲み物
Food and Drink

051 Ryokucha

緑茶

What is *ryokucha*?

Ryokucha, or green tea, is Japanese tea. It is made using a teapot just like Western tea, but we never add sugar or milk to green tea. There's also powdered green tea called *matcha*. *Matcha* is mixed with hot water to be drunk. *Matcha* is also used as an ingredient for sweets.

緑茶って何だろう？
緑茶は日本のお茶です。西洋のお茶と同じように急須を用いて入れますが、日本では緑茶に砂糖やミルクを入れることはありません。抹茶と呼ばれる粉末の茶もあります。抹茶は、お湯と混ぜて飲みます。抹茶は、お菓子の材料としても用いられます。

イラストで **くらべる！**

Ryokucha 緑茶 **VS** **Western tea** 西洋のお茶

Ryokucha を英語で説明してみよう

Q. **How is green tea different from Western tea?**

緑茶は西洋のお茶とどう違うの？

A. **The species of the tea plant is the same, but the process of preparing leaves is different. Western tea leaves are fermented by the enzyme contained in the leaves, so their color is blackish. Green tea leaves are heated soon after they have been picked to stop the fermentation.**

茶の木自体は同じなんだけど、茶葉の処理工程が違うんだ。西洋の茶葉は、葉に含まれる酵素を利用して発酵させているから、黒い色をしているでしょ。緑茶の茶葉は、摘んだ後すぐに加熱することで発酵を止めているんだ。

🟥Vocabulary 語句

green tea	緑茶	species	名 種
teapot	名 ティーポット、急須	process	名 工程
add A to B	A を B に加える	ferment	動 発酵させる
powdered	形 粉末状にした	enzyme	名 酵素
be mixed with ~	~と混ぜる	pick	動 ~を摘む
ingredient	名 材料	fermentation	名 発酵
sweets	名 お菓子		

052

Izakaya

居酒屋

What is *izakaya*?

Izakaya are Japanese taverns. They serve various kinds of food and drinks at reasonable prices. *Izakaya* are popular places for having drinking parties or after-hour drinking sessions among company colleagues. Many *izakaya* serve small dishes automatically. They are called *tsukidashi*, and are added to the bill as a kind of table charge.

居酒屋って何だろう？ 　居酒屋は日本式のタベルナです。いろいろな種類の食べ物や飲み物を安価に提供します。居酒屋は酒宴や、会社員が同僚同士で就業後の飲み会を開くのに人気の場所です。多くの居酒屋は注文せずとも小料理を出します。これは突き出しと呼ばれ、席料の一種として勘定書に加えられます。

イラストで **くらべる！**

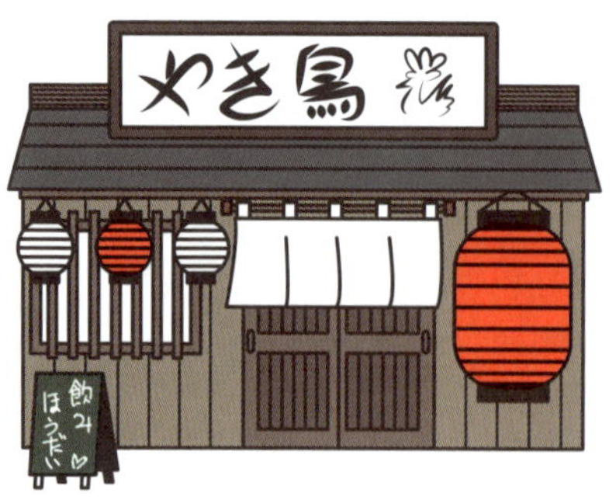

Izakaya を英語で説明してみよう

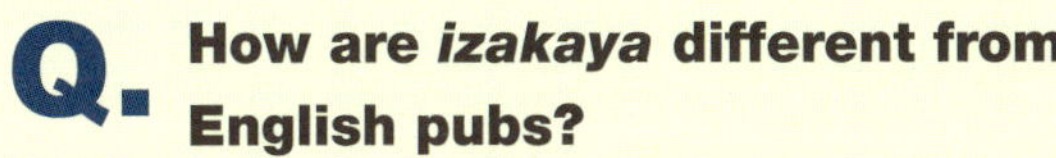

Q. **How are *izakaya* different from English pubs?**

居酒屋は、イギリスのパブとどう違う？

A. **Most *izakaya* serve a wide variety of cuisines from Japanese to Italian. A group of customers often share the dishes among themselves, so small plates are ready on the table. Also, customers usually pay upon order at English pubs, but at *izakaya*, the total bill is settled at the end.**

ほとんどの居酒屋は、和食からイタリアンまで幅広い料理を出すね。グループの客は料理をお互いに分け合うことが多いから、小皿がテーブルの上に用意してある。それにイギリスのパブでは、客が注文時に支払うのが普通だけど、居酒屋では勘定はまとめて最後に清算するんだ。

🎎 Vocabulary 語句

tavern	名 タベルナ（地中海地方に見られる飲み屋で、居酒屋の訳によく用いられる）	automatically	副 自動的に（ここでは、注文せずとも）
reasonable	形 手頃の	bill	名 勘定書
after-hour	形 就業後の	table charge	席料
drinking session	飲み会	cuisine	名 （ある地方に独特の）料理
colleague	名 同僚	share	動 ～を分け合う
		pay upon order	注文時に支払う
		settle	動 （勘定などを）清算する

137

053

Onigiri
おにぎり

What is *onigiri*?

Onigiri are rice balls. They are made by forming cooked rice into flattened triangular or round shapes. *Onigiri* are filled with tuna and mayonnaise, chopped Japanese pickles, dried bonito flakes, cooked kelp pieces, or a pickled plum, and are wrapped with a large sheet of dried nori seaweed.

おにぎりって何だろう？
おにぎりは、炊いたご飯を平たい三角形か丸い形にしたものです。おにぎりは、ツナマヨ、刻んだ漬物、鰹節、昆布の佃煮、梅干しなどの具が入れてあり、大きめのシート状の乾海苔で包んであります。

イラストで  くらべる！

Onigiri おにぎり **VS** **Sandwiches** サンドイッチ

Onigiri を英語で説明してみよう

Q. **Do you think *onigiri* are comparable to sandwiches?**

おにぎりは、サンドイッチに似ていると思う？

A. **Yes, I do. The ideas are very similar in that both are portable and eaten by hand — an ideal food as lunch or a snack. They both have grilled versions, too, although grilled *onigiri* are much simpler with no filling inside. Grilled *onigiri* are a popular menu item at *izakaya*.**

思うね。発想がよく似ていて、どちらも携帯できるし、手で食べられるよね。ランチや軽食に理想の食べ物だよ。それに、どちらも焼いたバージョンがあるしね。焼きおにぎりは具がなくて、ずっとシンプルだけどね。焼きおにぎりは居酒屋の人気メニューだよ。

第三章　食べ物・飲み物

🎎 Vocabulary 語句

flattened	形 平たくした		plum	名 梅の実
triangular	形 三角の		be wrapped with ~	~で包んである
round	形 丸い		seaweed	名 海藻
be filled with ~	~が中に入れてある		portable	形 携帯可能な
pickles	名 漬物		grilled	形 焼いた
bonito	名 カツオ		filling	名 （サンドイッチの具などの）詰め物
kelp	名 昆布			

054

Nabemono

鍋物

What is *nabemono*?

Nabemono refers to Japanese pot dishes. There are a wide variety of *nabemono*, using different materials and soup broths. *Yosenabe* is a typical *nabemono*, in which vegetables, meat and fish are simmered together in a shoyu-based broth. After the ingredients have been eaten, rice is often added to make it into porridge.

鍋物って何だろう？　鍋物は日本風の pot dishes を指します。鍋物には異なる材料や出汁を使う様々な種類があります。寄せ鍋は鍋物の代表で野菜、肉、魚などを醤油ベースの出汁で煮込みます。具材を食べ終えると、ご飯を加えて雑炊にすることがよくあります。

イラストでくらべる！

Nabemono 鍋物 **VS** **Stew** シチュー

Nabemono を英語で説明してみよう

Q. How is a *nabemono* different from a stew?

鍋物はシチューとどう違う？

A. A *nabemono* is cooked by the diners themselves at the table on a portable gas stove. People often share one large *nabemono* and take their favorite food and put it into their own small handled bowls. *Nabemono* can be a tool of communication, so it is regarded as an ideal party dish in winter.

鍋物は、食べる人が自らカセットコンロを使って食卓で調理するんだ。大きな鍋物をみんなで分け合うことが多くて、取っ手付きの自分の小さい器に好きな食べ物を取るんだ。鍋物は、コミュニケーションの道具にもなるから、冬の理想的なパーティ料理と思われているよ。

🎎 Vocabulary 語句

pot dish	鍋物料理	add A to B	A を B に加える
material	名 材料	porridge	名 雑炊、粥
broth	名 出汁	portable gas stove	携帯用ガスコンロ（＝カセットコンロ）
typical	形 代表的な		
simmer	動 ～をぐつぐつ煮る	small handled bowl	取っ手の付いた小さなうつわ（＝とんすい）
ingredient	名 具材		
		tool	名 道具

141

055 Oden
おでん

What is *oden*?

Oden is a dish of various ingredients simmered in a kelp broth seasoned with soy sauce. Popular ingredients include fish cakes, thickly cut daikon radish, *konnyaku* jelly, hard-boiled eggs, deep fried tofu, potatoes, and octopus. *Oden* is a popular winter dish, which is cooked at home or sold at convenience stores.

おでんって何だろう？ おでんは、様々な具を醤油で味付けした昆布出汁で煮込んだ料理です。人気の具には、練り物、厚切り大根、こんにゃく、固ゆで卵、揚げ豆腐、ジャガイモ、タコなどがあります。おでんは冬に人気の料理で、家庭で調理したり、コンビニで売られたりしています。

イラストで くらべる！

Oden おでん **VS** **Pot-au-feu** ポトフ

Oden を英語で説明してみよう

Q. **How is *oden* different from pot-au-feu?**

おでんとポトフはどう違う？

A. **They are very similar. In fact, oden is often called a Japanese version of pot-au-feu. One difference is that each *oden* ingredient is regarded as a separate food item, so at convenience stores or *izakaya*, each item often has its own price, and the customers can choose their favorite combination.**

両者はとても似ているね。実際、おでんは日本版ポトフと呼ばれることも多いし。1つの違いは、おでんの具は、それぞれが独立した食べ物みたいに思われていて、コンビニや居酒屋では、それぞれに値段が付けてあることが多く、客は自分の好みの組み合わせを選べるんだよ。

🧧 Vocabulary 語句

ingredient	名 材料、具材	**konnyaku jelly**	こんにゃく（近年、こんにゃく芋は、**konjac** の英語名で健康食品として知られるようになった）
simmer	動 〜をことこと煮る		
broth	名 出汁		
seasoned with 〜	〜で味付けした	**octopus**	名 タコ
fish cake	魚の練り物	**pot-au-feu**	名 （フランス語）ポトフ
daikon radish	大根	**separate**	形 個別の
		combination	名 組み合わせ

Shoyu

056

醬油

What is shoyu?

Shoyu is soy sauce. It is made from fermented soybeans and wheat. Shoyu is used for most Japanese dishes, along with miso, or fermented soybean paste, as a seasoning base or a dipping sauce. Today, there are many different kinds of shoyu available, from a less salty type to a thick, sweet type.

醬油って何だろう？

醤油は発酵させた大豆と麦から作られます。発酵した大豆の練り物である味噌と並んで、ほとんどの料理で味付けの基本や、つけ汁として使われます。今日では減塩醤油から濃くて甘い醤油まで、異なる種類の醤油がたくさん売られています。

イラストで くらべる！

Shoyu 醬油 VS Sauce ソース

発酵させた大豆と麦から作られる　　　　洋式の料理用

Shoyu を英語で説明してみよう

Q. Sauce refers to any kind of thick liquid served with other food, but in Japan you have a seasoning called "sauce". What is it?

食事と一緒に出される濃厚な液体なら何でもソースって呼ぶんだけど、日本には「ソース」と呼ばれる調味料があるよね。あれって何？

A. It's more specifically called "usutaa sauce". When Western dishes came to Japan, Japanese reinvented them to suit their taste. They also created a copy version of Worcestershire sauce, and named it "usutaa sauce". As opposed to shoyu used for Japanese dishes, this sauce is intended for Western-style dishes, being often simply called "sauce".

そのソースは、もっと正確に言うと「ウスターソース」と呼ばれるものだよ。西洋料理が日本にやってきたとき、日本人はそれらを自分の好みに合うように作り変えたんだ。また、Worcestershire sauce のコピー版も作って、それを「ウスターソース」と命名したんだ。日本料理に使われる醤油と対照的な存在として、このソースは洋式の料理用で、しばしば単に「ソース」と呼ばれるんだ。

Vocabulary 語句

soy sauce	醤油	Worcestershire sauce	ウスターシャーソース（イングランド発祥のソースで、日本のウスターソースのコピー元）
seasoning base	味付けの基本		
dipping sauce	つけ汁	as opposed to ～	～とは対照的に

145

057

Okonomiyaki

お好み焼き

What is *okonomiyaki*?

Okonomiyaki is a Japanese-style pancake made by grilling a mixture of batter and ingredients such as chopped seafood, meat and vegetables. It is seasoned with thick sauce and mayonnaise, and scattered with dried bonito flakes and green seaweed sprinkles. At some *okonomiyaki* restaurants, the customers themselves cook it on an iron plate embedded into the table.

お好み焼きって何だろう？　お好み焼きは、細切れの海産物、肉、野菜などを混ぜた生地を焼いて作られる、日本式のパンケーキです。濃い味のソースとマヨネーズで味付けして、鰹節と青のりを振りかけます。お好み焼きのお店には、テーブルに埋め込まれた鉄板で、客が自らお好み焼きを作るところもあります。

Okonomiyaki を英語で説明してみよう

Q. **How is *okonomiyaki* different from pancakes?**

お好み焼きはパンケーキとどう違う？

A. **Pancakes are thin, fluffy and sweet, but *okonomiyaki* is thicker, firmer and savory, and goes very well with alcoholic drinks such as beer. *Okonomiyaki* is voluminous, and is eaten as a meal. Although the cooking style and ingredients are different according to the region, I think *okonomiyaki* is more like a pizza.**

パンケーキは、薄くてふわふわして甘いけど、お好み焼きは分厚くって、それほどふわふわしてなくって、甘くないんだ。だからビールなんかのアルコール飲料とも相性がいいよ。お好み焼きは、ボリュームがあるから食事として食べるんだ。調理方法や使われる具材は、地域によって異なるけど、お好み焼きはピザに近いと思うね。

🎎 Vocabulary 語句

mixture	名 混ぜたもの	**embedded into ～**	～に埋め込まれた
batter	名 小麦粉と水と卵を混ぜたもの、（お好み焼きの）生地	**pancake**	名 ホットケーキ
		fluffy	形 ふわふわした
chopped	形 細切れにした	**savory**	形 甘くない（sweet の反意語）
scatter	動 ～を振りかける	**go well with ～**	～に合う
dried bonito flakes	削り節		
green seaweed sprinkles	青のりの振りかけ	**voluminous**	形 ボリュームがある（ボリューミーは和製英語）
iron plate	鉄板		

058

Bento

弁当

What is bento?

Bento refers to portable meals packed in special containers. They usually consist of cooked rice and several different kinds of side dishes. Ready-made bento sold at various stores are popular for their variety and reasonable prices. Home-made bento are also popular. They are often prepared to look beautiful to increase the joy of eating them.

弁当って何だろう？　弁当は、特殊な容器に詰めた携帯用の食事のことです。通常、ご飯と数種類のおかずからなっています。お店で売られている出来合いの弁当は、その多様さと手頃な値段で人気です。手作りの弁当も人気です。手作り弁当はしばしば、食べる楽しさが増すように見た目を美しく作ってあります。

イラストで くらべる！

Bento 弁当　VS　Brown bag lunch ブラウンバッグランチ

楽しませる要素が強い

携帯用の食事

Bento を英語で説明してみよう

Q. **How is bento different from a brown bag lunch?**

弁当は、ブラウンバッグランチとどう違う？

A. **I think bento is more entertaining. Bento boxes and related goods often bear anime characters. It is also common to depict those characters, animals and landscapes with bento contents. This type of bento is called *kyaraben*. *Kyaraben* is considered a way of communication between bento makers and their eaters.**

弁当は楽しませる要素が強いと思うね。弁当箱や関連グッズにはよくアニメのキャラが描かれていたりするし。そんなキャラや動物、風景なんかも弁当の中身で描くことも多いんだ。その手の弁当はキャラ弁と呼ばれていて、弁当を作る人と食べる人の間のコミュニケーションの手段と思われているんだ。

🟥 Vocabulary 語句

portable	形 携帯できる	joy	名 楽しみ
meal	名 （1回分の）食事	brown bag lunch	弁当、ブラウンバッグランチ（学校や職場などで食するための自家製の携帯ランチで、茶色の紙袋に入れることからの名称。**brown bag** で「持ち込みの飲食物」の意味もある）
pack	動 ～を詰め込む		
container	名 容器		
ready-made	形 出来合いの		
reasonable price	手頃な値段		
home-made	形 自家製の	bear	動 （絵などが）描かれている
prepare	動 ～を調理する、～を準備する	depict	動 ～を描く

059

Hashi

箸

What is *hashi*?

Hashi are chopsticks. Japanese chopsticks are usually made of wood or bamboo to avoid rice sticking to them, and have narrower tips to make it easier to pick up small or slippery items or to cut soft items. There are also disposable wooden chopsticks that are split into two before using.

箸って何だろう？　箸は chopsticks です。日本式の箸は、ご飯がくっつくのを避けるために、通常、木や竹で作られており、小さなものやつるつるしたものを取りやすいように、または柔らかいものを切りやすいように先が細くなっています。また、使う前に 2 本に分ける使い捨ての木製の箸もあります。

イラストで くらべる！

Hashi を英語で説明してみよう

Q. I think it's easier to eat rice bowl dishes with a spoon than with chopsticks. Why do you use chopsticks to eat them?

丼物は、箸よりもスプーンのほうが食べやすいと思うけど、どうして丼物を食べるのに箸を使うの？

A. The Japanese developed a custom of holding up the bowl and bring it closer to our mouth while eating. By doing so, we can eat any food by only using chopsticks, so the spoon culture didn't take hold in Japan. Meanwhile, it's thought bad-manners to eat from the bowl without holding it up.

日本人は食事のときに、お椀を持ち上げて口の近くまで持ってくるのが習慣になったんだ。そうすることで、どんな食べ物でも箸を使うだけで食べることができるから、スプーンの文化が根付かなかったんだ。一方で、お椀を持ち上げずに、お椀から食べるのは無作法とされているよ。

🎎 Vocabulary 語句

chopsticks	名 箸		item	名 品
bamboo	名 竹		disposable	形 使い捨ての
stick to ～	～にくっつく		split	動 ～を分ける
narrow	形 （棒などが）細い		hold up ～	～を持ち上げる
tip	名 先端		take hold	定着する
slippery	形 つるつるした		bad-manners	名 無作法

060 *Nomihodai*
飲み放題

What is *nomihodai*?

Nomihodai means all-you-can-drink. Most *izakaya* offer party menus including a two- to three-hour *nomihodai* service at fixed prices. The last order is usually taken 30 minutes before the time limit. The service is convenient for *izakaya* to increase the seat turnover, while the customers can enjoy drinking without worrying about the budget.

飲み放題って何だろう？ 飲み放題は all-you-can-drink の意味です。多くの居酒屋は、団体客を対象に、2〜3時間の飲み放題付きのパーティメニューを定額で提供します。ラストオーダーは通常、制限時間の30分前です。このサービスは、居酒屋にとって、客席回転率が高くなるので便利な一方、客は予算を気にせずに飲んで楽しむことができます。

イラストで **くらべる！**

Nomihodai 飲み放題 **VS** **Happy hour** ハッピーアワー

Nomihodai を英語で説明してみよう

Q. **In my country, happy hour is more common than *nomihodai*. Is it popular in Japan?**

自分の国では、飲み放題よりもハッピーアワーのほうがもっと一般的だけど、ハッピーアワーは日本では人気なの？

A. **Happy hour is becoming popular in Japan, although it usually starts a bit later at around 5 p.m. The government is now pressuring Japanese companies to shorten their employees' working hours, and I think happy hour can be a good incentive for them to leave their office earlier.**

ハッピーアワーは日本で人気になってきているよ。始まる時間がやや遅くて、普通 5 時ぐらいからだけどね。政府は今、日本の企業に、従業員の労働時間を短くするようにプレッシャーをかけているんだ。ハッピーアワーは、彼らがオフィスを早めに退社する良い動機になると思うな。

🔴 Vocabulary　語句

all-you-can-drink	名 飲み放題（食べ放題は、all-you-can-eat と言う）
fixed price	定額
order	名 注文
the time limit	制限時間
convenient	形 便利な

seat turnover	客席回転率
worry about 〜	〜について心配する
budget	名 予算
happy hour	ハッピーアワー（レストランやパブなどで酒類の割引を行う時間帯）
incentive	名 動機

061

Tempura

てんぷら

What is tempura?

Tempura is a traditional Japanese dish consisting of seafood and vegetables that have been battered and deep-fried. They are eaten with salt or after being dipped in a special sauce. They are also used as toppings for a rice bowl dish called *tendon* and noodle dishes like soba and udon.

てんぷらって何だろう？
てんぷらは、衣を付けて油揚げにした海産物や野菜からなる伝統的な日本料理です。塩を付けて、あるいは特別な汁に浸してから食べます。てんぷらは、天丼と呼ばれる丼物や、そばやうどんといった麺料理のトッピングとしても使われます。

イラストで くらべる！

Tempura てんぷら VS Fritters フリッター

サクサクしている

柔らかい

Tempura を英語で説明してみよう

Q. **How is tempura different from fritters?**

てんぷらは、フリッターとどう違う？

A. **The biggest difference is the batter. Fritter batter is made by adding meringue, so it gets soft when deep-fried. It is often seasoned, so fritters can be eaten without sauce. Tempura batter does not contain meringue, so it gets crispy when deep-fried. Tempura is often served with a shoyu-based dipping sauce.**

一番の違いは衣だね。フリッターの衣はメレンゲを加えて作られるから、揚げたときに柔らかくなるんだ。フリッターの衣は味付けしてあることが多いから、フリッターはソースなしでも食べられるよね。てんぷらの衣はメレンゲを使っていないから、揚げたときにサクサクになるんだ。てんぷらは、醤油ベースの漬け汁と一緒に出されることが多いよ。

🎎 Vocabulary 語句

tempura	名 てんぷら（英語では、tenpura ではなく、tempura と綴られる）
batter	動 ～に衣を付ける（名詞で使うと「衣」の意味）
deep-fry	動 ～を油揚げする
dip ～ in...	～を…に浸す

topping	名 トッピング（料理や食品の上に載せたり飾りとして振りかけたりするもの）
rice bowl dish	丼物
noodle dish	麺料理
meringue	名 メレンゲ（卵の白身を固く泡立てたもの）
crispy	形 サクサクした

155

062

Miso soup

味噌汁

What is miso soup?

Miso soup is a traditional Japanese soup. It is made by cooking various ingredients, mainly vegetables, in a broth seasoned with dried kelp or bonito, and adding miso to it. Popular ingredients include tofu and wakame seaweed. There are variations in taste depending on the type of miso used.

訳

味噌汁って何だろう？
味噌汁は、伝統的な日本のスープです。様々な具材、主に野菜を、昆布か鰹節で味付けした出汁で煮込み、味噌を加えて作ります。人気の具材には、豆腐や、海藻のワカメがあります。使われる味噌の種類によって、味に違いがあります。

イラストで くらべる！

Miso soup を英語で説明してみよう

Q. **How are miso soup and Western soup different?**

味噌汁と西洋のスープはどこが違う？

A. **The ways they are eaten are different. Western soup is often eaten before main dishes, but miso soup is eaten with rice, because it makes the rice tastier and nutritiously better-balanced. Also, the Japanese hold the bowl of miso soup, and sip the soup directly from it.**

食べ方が違うね。西洋のスープは主食の前に食べることが多いけど、味噌汁は、ご飯と一緒に出されるんだ。味噌汁は、ご飯の味や栄養バランスを良くしてくれるからね。それに、日本人は味噌汁の椀を手で持って、お椀から直接汁をすするんだ。

🎎 Vocabulary 語句

ingredient	名 材料	seaweed	名 海藻
broth	名 出汁	variation	名 違い
seasoned with ～	～で味付けをした	nutritiously	副 栄養の面で
kelp	名 昆布	better-balanced	形 バランスがより良い
bonito	名 カツオ		
add A to B	A を B に加える	sip	動 ～をすする

063

Tsukemono

漬物

What is tsukemono?

Tsukemono are Japanese pickles. They are made by pickling various vegetables such as daikon radishes, *hakusai*, cucumbers and eggplant in salt, soy sauce, miso or rice bran. Some are made by fermenting the ingredients. They are rich in vitamins and minerals, so are ideal complements to rice, the Japanese staple food.

漬物って何だろう？ 　漬物は日本版のピクルスです。様々な材料、主に野菜を塩、醤油、味噌、ぬかなどに漬けて作ります。材料を発酵させて作る漬物もあります。漬物はビタミンやミネラルに富むので、日本人の主食であるご飯を補完するための理想的な食べ物です。

イラストで **くらべる！**

Tsukemono 漬物 VS Pickles ピクルス

Tsukemono を英語で説明してみよう

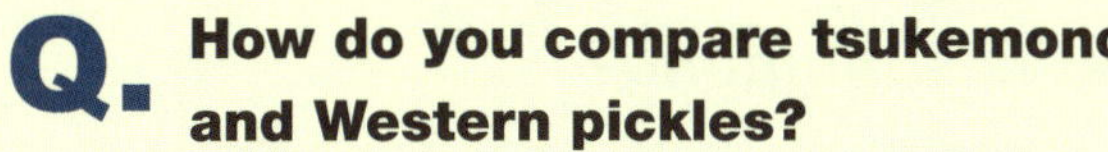

Q. **How do you compare tsukemono and Western pickles?**

漬物と西洋のピクルスを比べるとどう？

A. **Both have many different kinds, so it's difficult to compare, but generally speaking, Western pickles are sourer while tsukemono are saltier. Pickles are mainly used as a topping or a garnish, while tsukemono are mainly served as a side dish for rice or for alcoholic drinks.**

どちらもいろんな種類があるから比べるのは難しいけど、一般的に言うと、西洋のピクルスのほうが酸味が強いのに対し、漬物のほうが塩味が強いな。ピクルスは主に、トッピングや付け合わせに使われるのに対し、漬物は主に、ご飯のおかずやお酒のおつまみとして出されるよね。

🟥 Vocabulary 語句

pickle	名 ピクルス（通例 〜 s。野菜や果物などを酢や塩水に漬けた食品） 動 〜をピクルスにする	be rich in 〜	〜に富む
		ideal	形 理想的な
		complement to 〜	〜を補完するもの
		staple food	主食
cucumber	名 キュウリ	compare	動 〜を比べる
eggplant	名 ナス	sour	形 酸味が強い
rice bran	米ぬか	salty	形 塩味が強い
ferment	動 〜を発酵させる	topping	名 トッピング
ingredient	名 材料	garnish	名 付け合わせの食べ物

064

Sunomono
酢の物

What is *sunomono*?

Sunomono is a dish made by adding a vinegar sauce to seafood, vegetables and seaweed. A typical example is *kohaku-namasu*, which is made with thinly sliced daikon radish and carrots. Because the combination of red and white is thought auspicious in Japan, it is often served as a New Year dish.

酢の物って何だろう？

酢の物は、海産物、野菜、海藻などに合わせ酢を加えて作られる料理です。代表例は紅白なますで、千切りにした大根とニンジンで作られます。紅白の組み合わせは日本では縁起が良いとされるので、しばしば正月の料理として出されます。

タコとキュウリの酢の物

サーモンのマリネ

Sunomono を英語で説明してみよう

Q. **Is *sunomono* like marinated dishes?**

酢の物ってマリネに似ている？

A. Yes, it is similar, but *sunomono* is much simpler in taste because it doesn't use oil or spices. One aim of marinating food is to make it softer. In that sense, *nanbanzuke* might be similar. It is a dish of deep-fried fish marinated with vegetables and a spicy sweetened vinegar sauce.

似ているね。でも、酢の物は、油やスパイスは使わないから、味がもっとシンプルだね。食べ物をマリネにする目的の１つは、食べ物を柔らかくすることだよね。その意味で言うと、南蛮漬けが近いかな。南蛮漬けは、油で揚げた魚を、野菜とスパイスの利いた甘酢のソースでマリネにした料理だよ。

🎎 Vocabulary 語句

add A to B	A を B に加える	**carrot**	名	ニンジン
vinegar	名 酢	**combination**	名	組み合わせ
seaweed	名 海藻	**auspicious**	形	縁起の良い
thinly sliced	千切りにした	**marinated dish**		マリネ
daikon radish	ダイコン	**marinate**	動	～をマリネにする

065

Shochu
焼酎

What is shochu?

Shochu is a distilled alcoholic drink made from sweet potatoes, rice, barley or sugarcane. The so-called genuine shochu has a rich flavor, so is usually drunk on the rocks or mixed with iced or hot water, while other shochu with little flavor is usually drunk mixed with tea or juices.

焼酎って何だろう？
焼酎は、サツマイモ、米、大麦、サトウキビなどから造られる蒸留酒です。いわゆる本格焼酎は、豊かな風味があり、通常、ロックにして飲むか、氷水かお湯と混ぜるだけで飲みますが、香りがほとんどない他の焼酎は、通常、茶やジュースと混ぜて飲みます。

イラストで くらべる！

Shochu 焼酎 VS Vodka ウォッカ

Shochu を英語で説明してみよう

Q. **How is shochu different from vodka?**

焼酎は、ウォッカとどう違う？

A. **There are two types of shochu: a continuous distillation type, and a single distillation type. The former is similar to vodka, having little flavor of the original material. The latter is called genuine shochu and retains the flavor of the original material, like malt whisky. It is usually more expensive.**

焼酎には、連続蒸留で作られたものと単式蒸留で作られたものがあるんだ。前者はウォッカに似ていて、原材料の香りがほとんどないんだ。後者は、本格焼酎と呼ばれて、モルトウィスキーのように、原材料の風味が残っているんだ。こっちのほうが普通は高価だね。

🎎 Vocabulary 語句

distilled	形 蒸留された（「蒸留」は、発酵した原材料のもろみを加熱してアルコール成分を抽出すること）	vodka	名 ウォッカ
sweet potato	サツマイモ	continuous distillation	連続蒸留（もろみを連続的に蒸留しながら100パーセントに近いアルコールを取り出す製法）
barley	名 大麦		
sugarcane	名 サトウキビ	single distillation	単式蒸留（もろみを1〜数回蒸留して、原材料の風味を残してアルコールを抽出する製法。アルコール度数は連続蒸留よりも低くなる）
genuine	形 本物の、本格的な		
flavor	名 風味		
on the rocks	ロックで	malt whisky	モルトウィスキー
iced water	氷水		

066

Wasabi

わさび

What is wasabi?

Wasabi is horseradish. Native Japanese wasabi species is called *hon-wasabi*, literally genuine wasabi. Wasabi is used as a condiment for sushi and sashimi. It not only gives a hot and spicy flavor, but also helps keep food fresh due to its antibacterial properties. Wasabi is usually available in a paste or powder form.

わさびって何だろう？　わさびはホースラディッシュです。日本固有種のわさびは文字通り、本物のわさびの意味で本わさびと呼ばれます。すしや刺身の薬味に用いられます。辛くてピリッとした風味を出すだけでなく、抗菌効果があり食品を新鮮に保つのに役立ちます。普通、練り物や粉末状の製品として売られています。

イラストで くらべる！

Wasabi わさび VS Western horseradish 西洋わさび

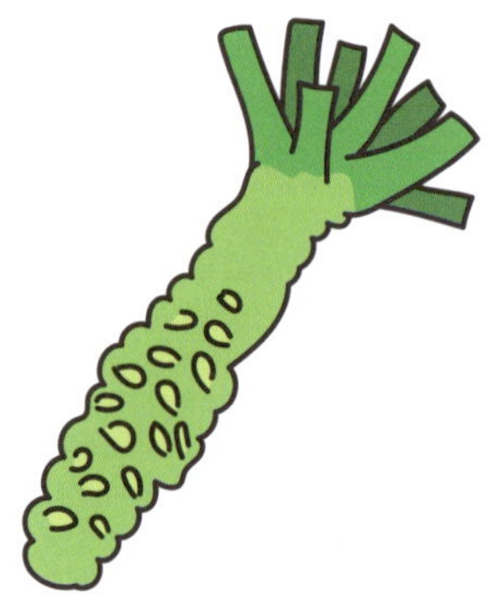

くらべてスッキリ！

Wasabiを英語で説明してみよう

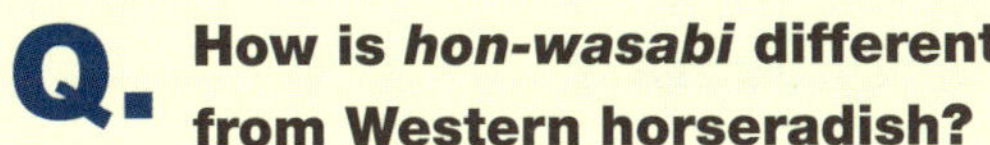

Q. How is *hon-wasabi* different from Western horseradish?

本わさびは、西洋わさびとどう違う？

A. *Hon-wasabi* is greenish whereas Western horseradish is yellowish, although the substances contained are very similar. Growing *hon-wasabi* is labor-intensive and costly, so most wasabi products use Western horseradish as their main ingredient, with a small amount of *hon-wasabi* added for flavoring.

本わさびが緑っぽいのに対し、西洋わさびは黄色っぽいね。含まれている成分はとても似ているけどね。本わさびの栽培は、たくさんの人手がかかってコストもかかるんだ。だから、ほとんどのわさび製品は、主要成分に西洋わさびを使って、少量の本わさびが風味づけに添加してあるんだよ。

Vocabulary 語句

horseradish	名 わさび
species	名 （動植物の）種
genuine	形 本物の
condiment	名 薬味
spicy	形 ピリッとする
flavor	名 風味
fresh	形 新鮮な
antibacterial property	抗菌効果（**property**は「効能」の意味）
paste	名 練り物
substance	名 物質
labor-intensive	形 たくさんの人手がかかる
costly	形 コストがかかる

Shojin ryori

精進料理

067

What is *shojin ryori*?

Shojin ryori is a vegetarian meal served for Buddhist monks. It contains no meat or fish based on the Buddhist prohibition of taking any life. It is especially important in Zen Buddhism because preparing and having *shojin ryori* is considered an important part of training. Some temples offer *shojin ryori* to visitors as well.

精進料理って何だろう？ 　精進料理は、仏僧に出される菜食です。仏教の不殺生戒に基づき、肉や魚を使っていません。精進料理は、特に禅宗において大切で、精進料理を調理したり食したりするのは修行の大切な一部分だとされています。参拝者にも精進料理を振る舞うお寺もあります。

イラストで くらべる！

Shojin ryori 精進料理 **VS** Western vegetarian meal 西洋の菜食

目的：煩悩を追い払う

菜食主義者用

Shojin ryori を英語で説明してみよう

Q. **How is *shojin ryori* different from Western vegetarian meals?**

精進料理は、西洋の菜食とどう違う？

A. *Shojin ryori* is aimed at driving away worldly desires, so it avoids vegetables having stronger smells like garlic and ginger that are thought to stimulate them. Besides, *shojin ryori* is a tool of training, so its eaters are not necessarily vegetarians. In fact, Buddhist monks are allowed to eat meat in Japan.

精進料理は、煩悩を追い払うことを目的としているから、煩悩を刺激すると思われる、ニンニクやショウガなどの臭いの強い野菜は避けるんだ。それに、精進料理は、精進の手段であって、食べる人が菜食主義者とは限らないんだ。事実、日本では、仏僧は肉食が許されているんだよ。

🟥 Vocabulary 語句

vegetarian meal	菜食	training	名 修行
Buddhist monk	仏僧、仏教の僧侶	drive away ~	～を追い払う
prohibition	名 禁止（ここでは、仏教の不殺生戒）	worldly desires	煩悩
		garlic	名 ニンニク
take life	命を奪う	ginger	名 ショウガ
Zen Buddhism	禅宗	stimulate	動 ～を刺激する
prepare	動 ～を調理する	tool	名 手段

068

Chuhai
酎ハイ

What is *chuhai*?

Chuhai is a kind of cocktail made by mixing shochu, a distilled alcoholic drink, with other drinks such as tea, soda and fruit juices. The name derives from the abbreviation of shochu highball, so originally it referred to shochu and soda, but later it came to mean shochu cocktails in general.

酎ハイって何だろう？　酎ハイは蒸留酒の焼酎と、茶、炭酸水、果汁などの他の飲み物とを混ぜて作ったカクテルの一種です。酎ハイという名前は、焼酎ハイボールの略語に由来するため、もともとは焼酎の炭酸割りを指していましたが、後に、焼酎を使ったカクテル全般を意味するようになりました。

イラストで くらべる！

Chuhai 酎ハイ VS Cocktails カクテル

シンプル

ソフトドリンクに
焼酎やウォッカを混ぜる

複数の果汁やリキュールや
蒸留酒を混ぜる

Q. **What are differences between *chuhai* and cocktails?**

酎ハイとカクテルの違いは？

A. *Chuhai* is simpler. It is a mixture of any kind of soft drink and shochu, or sometimes vodka, whereas a cocktail often mixes several different kinds of fruit juices, liqueurs and distilled drinks. Also, *chuhai* is often drunk with a meal, but cocktails are usually drunk before or after a meal.

酎ハイのほうがシンプルだよ。何らかのソフトドリンクに、焼酎、時にはウォッカを混ぜたものだけど、カクテルはよく複数の果汁やリキュールや蒸留酒を混ぜるよね。それに、酎ハイは、食事とともに飲むことが多いけど、カクテルは食前・食後に飲むのが普通だよね。

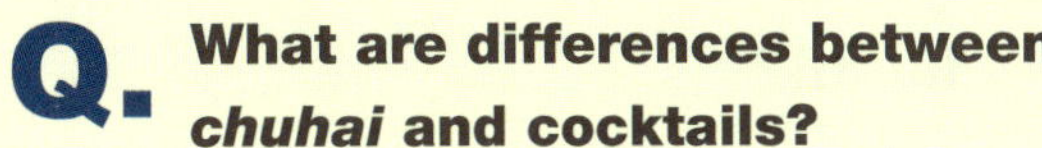

🎴 Vocabulary 語句

cocktail	名 カクテル	highball	名 ハイボール（ウィスキーをソーダやジンジャーエールで割った飲み物）
mix A with B	A と B を混ぜる		
distilled alcoholic drink	蒸留酒		
soda	名 炭酸水	〜 in general	〜全般
derive from 〜	〜に由来する	mixture	名 混合物
abbreviation	名 略語	liqueur	名 リキュール

069

Dashi

出汁

What is dashi?

Dashi is a Japanese soup broth, which is used as a base for miso soup and simmered dishes. Dashi is made by soaking dried bonito flakes or dried kelp in simmering water. Kelp dashi is basically suited to meat or fish dishes, and bonito dashi to vegetable dishes.

出汁って何だろう？

出汁は、日本のスープブロスで、味噌汁や煮物のベースとして使われます。鰹節や昆布の干物を煮えているお湯に入れて作ります。昆布出汁は、基本的に肉料理や魚料理に合い、鰹出汁は野菜料理に合います。

イラストで くらべる！

Dashi 出汁 **VS** Western broth 西洋のブロス

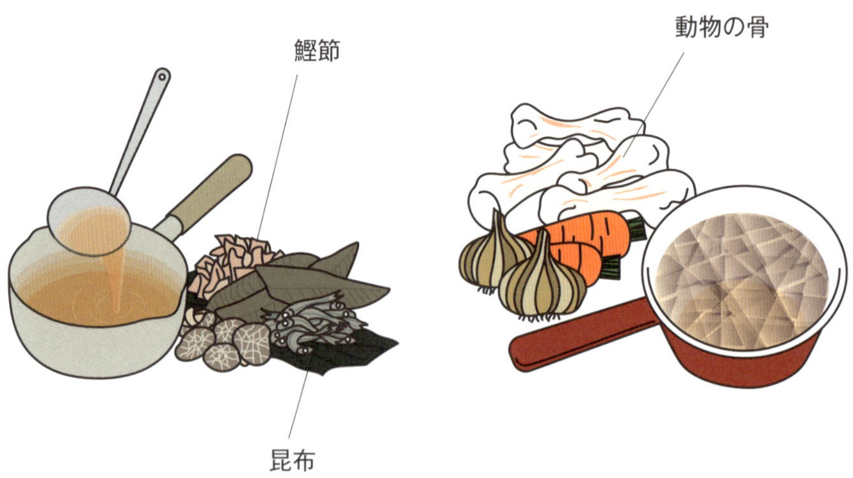

Dashi を英語で説明してみよう

Q. How is dashi different from Western broth?

出汁は、西洋のブロスとどう違う？

A. Western broth is usually made by simmering ingredients for a long time. Also, it often uses animal bones, so it contains a lot of gelatin. In making dashi, ingredients are simmered only for a short time to extract only umami substances, so it has a very light taste and contains no gelatin.

西洋のブロスは、普通、材料を長時間煮込んで作るよね。それに、動物の骨を使うことが多いから、ゼラチンをたくさん含んでいるよね。出汁を作るときには、うまみ成分だけを取り出すために、材料はほんの短い時間しか煮込まないから、出汁はとても味が薄くて、ゼラチンも含んでいないんだ。

🎎Vocabulary 語句

broth	名 ブロス（肉と骨・海産物・野菜などを長時間煮込んだスープやソースの素。フランス料理のフォンやブイヨンなど）
simmered dish	煮物
soak A in B	A を B に浸す

bonito	名 鰹
flake	名 薄片
kelp	名 昆布
simmering water	煮えているお湯
be suited to ～	～に合う
gelatin	名 ゼラチン
extract	動 ～を抽出する

070

Kaiseki

懐石

What is *kaiseki*?

Kaiseki is a traditional Japanese multicourse meal. It originated as a light meal served at a tea gathering, but later developed into haute cuisine served at ryokan and exclusive restaurants. It consists of a variety of dishes using vegetables, meat and fish, which are served in a fixed order.

懐石って何だろう？

懐石は、伝統的な日本のフルコース料理です。もともと茶会で出される軽い食事として発祥しましたが、後に、旅館や料亭で出される高級料理へと発達しました。懐石は、野菜、肉、魚を使った様々な料理からなり、決まった順番で出されます。

イラストで **くらべる！**

Japanese food 日本料理 **VS** **Western food** 西洋料理

いろいろな素材、色、形、感触の
皿や鉢

おそろいの丸い皿

Japanese food を英語で説明してみよう

Q. How do you compare the Japanese food presentation with Western food presentation?

日本料理の盛り付け方と西洋料理の盛り付け方を比べると？

A. In the West, food is presented on uniform round plates, but Japanese food is served using plates and bowls of various materials, colors, shapes and textures. Also, food is arranged in a symmetrical form in the West, whereas Japanese food is arranged asymmetrically to look more natural.

西洋では、料理はおそろいの丸いお皿に盛るけど、日本料理は、いろんな素材、色、形、感触の皿や鉢を使って出されるね。それに、西洋では、料理が左右対称形に盛られるけど、日本料理は、もっと自然に見えるように、左右非対称に盛られるんだ。

第三章 ✿ 食べ物・飲み物

🎎 Vocabulary 語句

multicourse meal	フルコースの料理（full-course meal とも）	in a fixed order	決まった順番で
originate as ～	～として発祥する	food presentation	料理の盛り付け
meal	名（1回分の）食事	uniform	形 おそろいの
tea gathering	茶会	texture	名 感触
haute cuisine	高級料理（フランス語より）	arrange	動 ～を盛り付ける
exclusive	形 高級な	symmetrical	形 左右対称の
		asymmetrically	副 左右非対称に

Sushi

071

すし

What is sushi?

Sushi is a dish of vinegared rice. The most common type of sushi in Japan is nigiri zushi. It is a dish of small hand-rolled balls of vinegared rice topped with various ingredients, usually raw fish. Some of the popular toppings include tuna, salmon, and yellowtail.

すしって何だろう？

すしは、酢飯を使った料理です。日本で最も一般的なすしは握りずしです。握りずしは酢飯を手で小さく丸めて、様々な具材（ネタ）をのせたもので、よく見られる具材は生魚です。人気のネタには、まぐろ、サーモン、ブリなどがあります。

イラストで **くらべる！**

Sushi を英語で説明してみよう

Q. **I like California rolls. Are they popular in Japan, too?**

僕はカリフォルニアロールが好きだけど、日本でも人気なの？

A. **Yes, they are. They are similar to maki zushi. In California rolls, a sheet of nori is used to wrap the ingredients in the center, while in maki zushi the whole roll of vinegared rice with the ingredients in the center is wrapped with a sheet of nori.**

うん、人気だよ。カリフォルニアロールは、巻きずしに近いね。カリフォルニアロールでは、真ん中にある具材を包むのにシート状の海苔を使うけど、巻きずしでは、具材を中心に入れた筒状の酢飯全体をシート状の海苔で巻くんだ。

🟥 Vocabulary 語句

vinegared rice	酢飯（すし飯）、ここでは、シャリ	**topping**	名 トッピング、上にのせるもの、ここでは、ネタ
common	形 一般的な、よくある	**tuna**	名 マグロ
hand-rolled	形 手で丸めた	**salmon**	名 サケ
topped with ~	~をのせた	**yellowtail**	名 ブリ
ingredient	名 （料理などの）材料	**wrap**	動 ~を包む
raw fish	生魚（**fish** はここでは不可算名詞。可算名詞として **a raw fish** とすると、生魚丸1匹の意味になる）	**the whole roll**	筒状のもの全体

第三章　食べ物・飲み物

Q. **What are some other types of popular sushi in Japan?**

日本で人気のすしには、他にどんな種類のものがあるの？

One is *inarizushi*. A small ball of vinegared rice is wrapped with deep-fried tofu seasoned with soy sauce and sugar. Another popular type of sushi is *chirashizushi*. It is a dish of vinegared rice mixed with various ingredients including fish and vegetables. It is usually topped with bits of fried egg and nori seaweed. *Chirashizushi* is often prepared for special occasions such as festivals.

１つは稲荷ずしだね。小さく丸めた酢飯を、醤油と砂糖で味付けした揚げ豆腐でくるんであるんだ。また別の人気のすし料理にちらし寿司があるね。ちらし寿司は、魚や野菜などのいろんな具材を酢飯に混ぜ込んであるんだ。普通は、トッピングに細切れの焼き卵や海苔がのせてあるよ。ちらし寿司は、よく、お祭りなどの特別な行事のために作られるんだ。

Q. Is it safe to eat raw fish?

生魚って食べても安全なの？

A. Yes, it is. In many other cultures, eating raw fish is thought dangerous because of possible food poisoning, but it's different in Japan. In the preparation of dishes using raw fish like sushi and sashimi, special care is taken to keep the ingredients fresh. Also, vinegar and wasabi Japanese horseradish, which is used as a condiment, can help prevent the propagation of bacteria. As long as it is properly prepared, you don't have to worry about the safety at all.

安全だよ。他の多くの文化圏では、食中毒にかかる可能性があるんで生魚を食べるのは危険だと思われているけど、日本では違うんだ。すしや刺身といった生魚の調理には、材料を新鮮に保つための特別の注意が払われているんだ。それに、酢や、薬味に使われる本わさびは、バクテリアの繁殖を防ぐ役割を果たしている。きちんと調理されてさえいれば、安全に関しては全く心配しなくていいよ。

第三章 🌸 食べ物・飲み物

🎎 Vocabulary 語句

deep-fried	形 油で揚げた	keep ~ fresh	~を新鮮に保つ
seasoned with ~	~で味付けをした	condiment	名 薬味
mixed with ~	~と混ぜた	prevent	動 ~を防ぐ
bits of ~	~の細切れ	propagation	名 増殖
occasion	名 行事	properly	副 適切に
food poisoning	食中毒	worry about ~	~について心配する

072

Soba

そば

What is soba?

Soba are noodles made from blends of wheat and buckwheat flours. They are served either cold with a dipping sauce or warm in a hot broth topped with various ingredients such as tempura, a raw egg, or seasoned deep-fried tofu. Soba are considered a symbol of longevity for their thin long shape.

そばって何だろう？　そばは、小麦粉とそば粉のブレンドから作られる麺です。冷たくして漬け汁と一緒に出したり、温かくして熱い汁に入れて、てんぷら、生卵、きつねなど、いろいろなトッピングをのせて出したりします。そばは、その細くて長い形から、長寿の象徴とされています。

Udon うどん **VS** **Pasta** パスタ

Udon を英語で説明してみよう

Q. **Is there food similar to pasta in Japan?**

パスタに似た食べ物って日本にある？

A. **Udon noodles might be similar to spaghetti. Udon is made from wheat flour, and is eaten either warm or cold just like soba. The flavors and textures are quite different according to the region where they are made. These days, pasta dishes using udon instead of spaghetti are becoming popular.**

うどんはスパゲティに近いかもね。うどんは小麦粉から作られていて、そばと同じように、温かくするか冷たくするかして食べるんだ。味や歯ごたえは作られている地域によってかなり違うよ。最近では、うどんをスパゲティの代わりに使ったパスタ料理が人気になってきているんだ。

🙂 Vocabulary 語句

blend	名 ブレンド（**2**つ以上のものを、それぞれの個性が生きるように混ぜたもの）
wheat flour	小麦粉
buckwheat flour	そば粉
serve ~ cold [warm]	～を冷たくして［温かくして］出す
dipping sauce	つけ汁
broth	名 だし汁

topped with ~	～がのせてある
ingredient	名 材料
seasoned	形 味付けした
deep-fried	形 油で揚げた
symbol	名 象徴
longevity	名 長寿
thin	形 細い
flavor	名 味、風味
texture	名 歯ざわり、噛み応え

A. Ramen uses Chinese noodles, whereas soba uses buckwheat noodles. Soup and dipping sauce for soba are shoyu-based, but ramen soup is usually made by adding shoyu-, miso- or salt-based seasonings to thick broths made from chicken, pork, or fish, so it is usually oilier. Like soba, various toppings are used for ramen, but those unique to ramen include slices of roast pork, boiled eggs and pickled bamboo shoots. Ramen is more diverse, with each region having its original kind.

ラーメンは中華麺を使うのに対し、そばは蕎麦麺を使うんだ。そばのつゆや漬けつゆは、醤油味だけど、ラーメンのスープは、醤油、味噌、塩などをベースにした調味料を、鶏、豚、魚などから作っただし汁に加えて作られるから、普通、そばのつゆよりも脂っこいね。そばと同じように、ラーメンにもいろんな具材をのせるけど、ラーメン独特というと、チャーシュー、ゆで卵、メンマなどがあるね。ラーメンはそばより多様で、それぞれの地域に独自の種類のラーメンがあるよ。

Q. Many people make slurping sounds when eating soba and ramen. Isn't it considered bad manners?

そばやラーメンを食べるときに、多くの人が、すする音を立てるよね。あれってマナーが悪いって思われないの？

A. No, it isn't in Japan. Soba noodles have a distinctive aroma, so some people say by slurping the noodles together with air, they can better enjoy the aroma. Another reason is that soba and ramen are usually served in very hot soup, so slurping helps cool the noodles. In addition, by slurping the noodles, you can take in more soup or sauce with them, which makes them tastier. However, slurping Western noodles like spaghetti is considered bad manners.

日本では思われないんだ。そばの麺は独特な香りがあって、麺と一緒に空気を吸い込むことで、その香りをより楽しめるという人がいるよ。別の理由として、そばやラーメンはとても熱いつゆに入れて出されるから、すすることで、麺を冷やすことができるんだ。それに、麺をすすると、つゆや漬けつゆをより多く吸い込むことができるから、美味しくなるんだ。ただし、スパゲティのような西洋の麺料理をすするのは無作法と思われているよ。

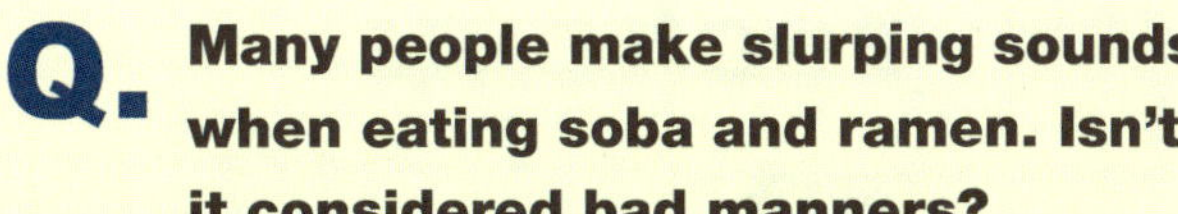 Vocabulary 語句

seasoning	名 調味料		bad manners	悪いマナー（manners はこの意味では複数形）
roast pork	チャーシュー		distinctive	形 独特の
pickled bamboo shoot	メンマ、シナチク		aroma	名 香り
diverse	形 多様な		take in 〜	〜を取り込む
slurping sound	すする音		tasty	形 美味しい

073

Yoshoku

洋食

What is *yoshoku*?

Yoshoku is a hybrid of Western and Japanese dishes. When Japan modernized in the late 19th century, many Western dishes came to Japan, and Japanese chefs arranged them to suit the Japanese taste, resulting in the creation of *yoshoku*. Typical examples include curry, spaghetti, omelet and rice, and pork cutlets.

洋食って何だろう？ 洋食は、西洋と日本の料理が合体した料理です。19世紀末に日本が近代化した折、多くの西洋料理が日本にもたらされ、日本人の料理人はそれらを日本人の好みに合うように工夫し、洋食を創作することになりました。代表的な例にはカレー、スパゲティ、オムライス、ポークカツレツなどがあります。

イラストで くらべる！

Japanese curry 日本のカレー **VS** **Indian curry** インド式カレー

Japanese curry を英語で説明してみよう

Q. **How is Japanese curry different from Indian curries?**

日本式のカレーは、インドのカレーとどう違う？

A. Indian curries were introduced to Britain in the 18th century, and developed into English-style curry. It came to Japan in the 19th century and developed in its own way. Japanese curry is thicker and milder so as to go well with Japanese rice, which is stickier and moister when cooked than Indica rice often used for Indian curries.

インドのカレーは 18 世紀に英国に伝わり、英国式カレーに発達したんだ。それが 19 世紀に日本に伝わって、独自に発達したんだよ。インドのカレーによく使われるインディカ米よりも、炊いたときに粘り気があってしっとりしている日本の米によく合うように、日本式のカレーは、とろみがあって甘めなんだ。

🧧Vocabulary 語句

hybrid	形	ハイブリッドの、混成の
modernize	動	近代化する
suit	動	～に合わせる
taste	名	好み
result in ~		～の結果になる
curry	名	カレー（日本式のものは curry and rice「カレーライス」と呼ばれる）
spaghetti	名	スパゲティ（ここでは、日本発祥の「ナポリタン」を指す）
omelet and rice		オムライス（omelet and rice という合成語を略したもの）

cutlet	名	カツレツ（肉を揚げたり焼いたりしたもの。pork cutlet は日本の「ポークカツレツ」を指す合成語。味噌汁と漬物と一緒に出すと和食として「とんかつ」と呼ばれる）
thick	形	とろみのある
mild	形	甘い、辛くない、刺激性の少ない
go well with ~		～に合う
sticky	形	粘り気のある
moist	形	しっとりした
Indica rice		インディカ米（タイ米など、炊いても粘り気がない長粒の米）

Q. **What are the characteristics of traditional Japanese cuisine?**

伝統的な和食の特徴は何？

A. **When Japanese cuisine was registered as Intangible Cultural Heritage, several of its characteristics were highly valued. First, it uses various fresh ingredients, and tries to enhance the natural taste of each ingredient. Second, it is nutritionally well-balanced and healthy, containing less fat. Third, its arrangement represents the beauty of nature and seasonal changes. Finally, it is closely related to traditional events and people's everyday customs.**

和食が無形文化遺産に登録されたとき、和食のいくつかの特徴が高く評価されたんだ。まず、和食は様々な新鮮な素材を使い、それぞれの素材が持つ自然の味を高めようとするんだ。第2に、和食は、脂肪分が少なく、栄養バランスに優れて健康に良いということ。第3に、和食の盛り付けが自然の美しさや四季の変化を表していること。最後に、和食が伝統行事や人々の生活習慣と緊密に結びついていることだね。

Q. I had *tonkatsu*, and it was very good. But is it a *washoku* or *yoshoku*?

とんかつを食べたけど、とても美味しかった。でも、とんかつは和食なの、洋食なの？

A. *Tonkatsu* is a dish of pork cutlet, so it was originally a kind of *yoshoku*, but many *tonkatsu* restaurants serve the dish in a Japanese style, along with miso soup and Japanese pickles, so *tonkatsu* is regarded as a *washoku*. An interesting distinction between *washoku* and *yoshoku* is whether the material names are Japanese or loan words. For example, ton of *tonkatsu* is a Japanese word meaning "pork", although *katsu* is a loan word from "cutlet", so *tonkatsu* can be classified as *washoku*.

とんかつはポークカツレツの料理だから、もともとは洋食の一種だったんだ。でも多くのとんかつ料理店では、とんかつを味噌汁と香の物と組み合わせて和式に提供しているから、とんかつは和食だと思われているね。和食と洋食の面白い区別の仕方は、材料の名前が日本語か外来語かという点があるんだ。例えば、とんかつの「かつ」は「カツレツ」から来た外来語だけど、「とんかつ」の「とん」は豚を意味する日本語なんだ。だから、とんかつは和食に分類することができるね。

🎎 Vocabulary 語句

be registered as ~	～として登録される		fat	名 脂肪分
Intangible Cultural Heritage	無形文化遺産		be related to ~	～と関連のある
			Japanese pickles	漬物
value	動 ～を重要だとする		loan word	外来語
enhance	動 ～を高める		be classified as ~	～に分類される

074

Sake
日本酒

What is sake?

Sake is a fermented alcoholic drink made from rice. Sake is drunk either chilled or warmed. Sake is an important offering to Shinto deities, and is used for various rituals like festivals and wedding ceremonies. There are local sake brands all over Japan, and ones from famous rice-producing areas are especially popular.

日本酒って何だろう？

酒は米から作られる醸造酒です。冷たくして、または、温めて飲まれます。酒は神道の神への大切な捧げものの１つで、祭りや結婚式などの儀式で用いられます。日本中に地方の酒のブランドがあり、有名米どころのブランドは特に人気です。

イラストで くらべる！

Sake 日本酒 VS Wine ワイン

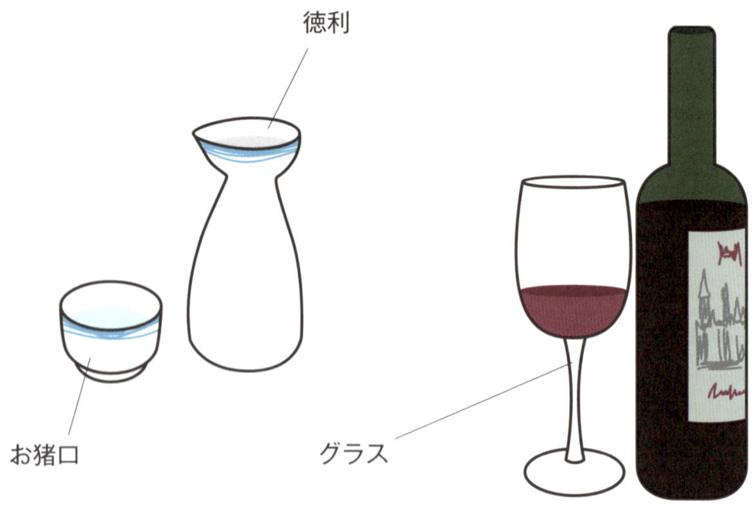

Sake を英語で説明してみよう

Q. **How is the process of sake making different from wine making?**

酒造りは、ワイン造りとどう違う？

A. **Wine is made by fermenting sugar contained in grapes by yeast, but because rice contains no sugar, the starch in rice grains is converted by koji mold into sugar, which is fermented by yeast into alcohol. Also, in sake making, polishing rice grains is important to remove unwanted substances from their surface.**

ワインは、ブドウに含まれる糖分をイースト菌で発酵させて造られるけど、米は糖分を含まないから、米のでんぷんを麹菌で糖に変えたうえで、できた糖をイースト菌でアルコールへと発酵させるんだ。また、酒の製造では、米粒の表面から不要な物質を取り除くために、精米することが大切なんだよ。

Vocabulary 語句

fermented	形 発酵された		yeast	名 イースト菌
chilled	形 冷たくされた		starch	名 でんぷん
offering	名 捧げもの（神道では神饌と呼ばれる）		be converted into ～	～に変えられる
deity	名 神		mold	名 カビ（麹菌はカビの一種）
ritual	名 儀式		polish	動 ～を磨く
rice-producing area	米の生産地		substance	名 物質

Q. **Are there different types of sake in terms of taste, quality and price?**

酒は、味や品質や価格などに関して違った種類があるの？

A. **Yes, there are. The taste is different depending on how much sugar and acid the sake contains. Sake with less sugar and more acid usually tastes drier. Quality usually depends on the rice polishing rate called *seimai-buai*, which is indicated by the percentage of the rice grains remaining, so generally speaking, the lower the rate is, the higher the quality. The prices vary depending on the quality, from premium sake made with selected materials and intensive labor, to cheap table sake containing added alcohol and flavor adjusting additives.**

うん、あるよ。味は、酒がどれだけ糖と酸を含んでいるかによって異なるね。糖分が少なくって酸度が高いものは辛口ということになる。品質は普通、精米歩合と呼ばれる、米の精米の割合で決まるね。精米歩合は、残留する米粒の割合で示すから、一般的に言うと、精米歩合が低ければ低いほど、品質が高いことになる。価格は、品質によって様々。厳選された材料で手間をかけて作った高級酒から、添加アルコールや味を調整するための添加物を含んだ安い低ランクの酒までね。

What are *ginjo* and *daiginjo*?

吟醸や大吟醸って何？

A. **They are categories indicating the quality of sake based on the rice polishing rates. *Daiginjo* refers to the highest-grade sake with the polishing rate of lower than 50 percent. *Ginjo* refers to the second-grade sake with the rate of 50 to 60 percent. The third-grade sake is called *hon-jozo*, with the rate of 60 to 70. Even premium sake often contains a little amount of added alcohol to enhance the taste. The product containing no added alcohol is called *junmai-shu*, meaning pure rice sake.**

精米歩合に基づいて酒の品質を示す分類なんだ。大吟醸は、精米歩合が 50 パーセント以下の最高級の酒のこと。吟醸は、精米歩合が 50 パーセントから 60 パーセントの二番目の等級の酒のこと。三番目の等級の酒は、本醸造と呼ばれて、精米歩合が 60 パーセントから 70 パーセント。高級酒であっても、味を良くするために、添加アルコールを少しだけ含んでいるものがあるんだ。添加アルコールを全く含まないものは、純粋な米の酒の意味で、純米酒と呼ばれるんだ。

🟥 Vocabulary 語句

acid	名 酸		intensive labor	多大な労力を必要とする
dry	形 （酒が）辛口の 〈⇔ sweet 形 （酒が）甘口の〉		table	形 食卓用の（ワインなどでは、しばしば低品質の製品を意味する）
polish	動 ～を磨く		additive	名 添加物
rice grain	米粒		category	名 分類
premium	形 高級の		grade	名 等級
selected	形 厳選された		enhance	動 ～を向上させる

Osechi

075

お節

What is *osechi*?

Osechi are traditional special dishes prepared for the New Year. They consist of various foods symbolizing happiness, longevity and prosperity, and are often served packed in layered square boxes called *jubako*. These days more people buy ready-made *osechi* at department stores instead of preparing them on their own.

お節って何だろう？ お節は、正月のために用意する伝統的な特別料理です。お節は、幸福、長寿、繁栄などを象徴する様々な食べ物からなっており、しばしば、重箱と呼ばれる重ねた四角の箱に詰めて出します。最近では、自分たちで作るよりも、作り置きのお節をデパートで買う人が多くなっています。

イラストで **くらべる！**

Osechi お節 **VS** **Dishes for Thanksgiving** 感謝祭の料理

Osechi を英語で説明してみよう

Q. In America, people prepare special dishes for Thanksgiving. Are they similar in concept to *osechi*?

アメリカでは、感謝祭のために特別料理を用意するけど、概念的にお節と似ている？

A. Yes, I think their cultural meanings are similar. Both are specially prepared for families to enjoy together to celebrate the occasion. One interesting aspect of osechi is that each food item symbolizes something. For example, *kurikinton*, a mixture of mashed chestnuts and sweet potatoes, looks like gold, symbolizing wealth.

そうだね、文化的な意味合いは似ているよね。どちらも、行事のお祝いとして、家族が一緒に楽しめるように特別に準備するからね。1つ、お節の面白いところは、それぞれの食べ物が何かを象徴しているところなんだ。例えば、栗とサツマイモをすりつぶして混ぜた栗きんとんは、金に似ているから、富を象徴しているとかね。

🎎 Vocabulary 語句

prepare	動 ～を用意する、～を調理する	layered boxes	複数の層になった箱
(the) New Year	正月、新年（the は、あってもなくてもよい）	ready-made	形 作り置きの
symbolize	動 ～を象徴する	department store	デパート
longevity	名 長寿	on one's own	自分で
prosperity	名 繁栄	Thanksgiving	名 感謝祭
pack	動 ～を詰める	mash	動 ～をすりつぶす
		chestnut	名 栗
		sweet potato	サツマイモ

A. Yes, they do. Shrimps symbolize longevity because their curved bodies are associated with old people. A dish using kelp symbolizes joy because the Japanese name of kelp *kobu* is a pun on a Japanese term *yorokobu* meaning "to be delighted". And black beans symbolize industriousness. Their Japanese name *kuromame* is a pun with a Japanese phrase *mameni-hataraku*, literally meaning "to work hard", which implies people's wish to stay healthy.

うん、あるよ。エビは長寿の象徴だね。エビの曲がった体はお年寄りを連想させるからね。昆布を使った料理は喜びを象徴するんだ。昆布を意味する日本語の「コブ」は、日本語の喜びや幸せを意味する「喜ぶ」と語呂が合うからね。黒豆は勤勉を象徴するんだ。日本名の「クロマメ」は、日本語の「まめに働く」という表現と語呂が合っていて、文字通りの意味では、「よく働く」だけど、健康でいることを願う気持ちを示しているんだ。

Q. **What are the origins of *osechi*?**

お節の起源は？

A. *Osechi* is said to have been developed from banquet meals served at court events. It gradually spread among common people, and became special dishes for the New Year. Later, *osechi* developed into a kind of preserved meal consisting of foods lasting longer based on the idea that during the New Year, Shinto deities visit each household, and we need to have food with them avoiding working in the kitchen during their stay.

お節は、宮廷儀式で出された宴会料理から発達したと言われているよ。それが次第に庶民の間に広まって、正月の特別料理になったんだ。後になって、正月には神道の神が各家庭にやって来るから、神様がいる間は台所で働くのを避けて神様と一緒に食事をするべきという考えに基づいて、お節は、日持ちのする食べ物で構成される、一種の保存食へと発達したんだ。

🍡 Vocabulary 語句

longevity	名 長寿		stay healthy	健康でいる
curved	形 曲がった		banquet meal	宴会料理
be associated with ～	～を連想させる		court event	宮廷行事
pun on [with] ～	～との語呂		preserved meal	保存食
be delighted	喜ぶ		last long	日持ちのする
industriousness	名 勤勉さ		deity	名 神
imply	動 ～を暗示する			

江戸幕府か徳川幕府か？

　日本文化を英語で紹介する時、固有名詞の扱い方で迷うことがあります。例えば、江戸幕府（1603 〜 1867 年）は徳川幕府とも呼ばれますが、一般に歴史の教科書では江戸幕府の呼称を用いています。ところが、英語では、the Tokugawa Shogunate と呼ばれるのが一般的です。shogunate は「幕府」を英語化した語で、「shogun（将軍）の政府」という意味から作られたものです。そのため、固有名詞にする場合、「江戸」よりも「徳川」のほうがふさわしい気がします。ちなみに、shogunate は一般名詞ですが、the Tokugawa Shogunate は固有名詞であるため、shogunate の s は大文字にすることが多いようです。

　室町幕府（1336 〜 1573 年）は、江戸幕府という名称同様、京都室町に政務所があったことからその名があります。歴史上では、室町に政務所を移したのは第三代将軍の義満ですが、初代将軍の尊氏までさかのぼって、室町幕府と呼ばれます。こちらは、英語表記ですと、the Muromachi Shogunate と the Ashikaga Shogunate が半々ぐらいで用いられています。まだ日本文化が詳しく知られる前に世界に名を知られた徳川と、その後、日本史の考察が進む中で知られるようになった足利の知名度の差かと思われます。

　さて、鎌倉幕府（1185 ［1192 とも］ 〜 1333 年）ですが、こちらは、the Kamakura Shogunate が一般的です。というのも、初代将軍の源頼朝の後、源氏は三代（頼朝―頼家―実朝）で滅びてしまい、以後、将軍は京都の摂関家や皇室から迎えるようになったため、the Minamoto Shogunate という名称が合わないからです。このように、日本文化を英語で説明するには、背景をよく理解していないと一貫性を欠く説明になってしまうことが多々ありますので、しっかりした考証や実際の用例などの検証が大切です。

歴史・観光
History and Tourism

 vs 

076

Ninja

忍者

What are ninja?

Ninja were secret agents in pre-modern Japan. They engaged in combat, intelligence activities, sabotage and assassination, using various weapons and skills. In the Edo Period, they became more like the government spies, and secretly monitored the actions of feudal lords. They disappeared with the end of samurai reign.

忍者って何だろう？
忍者は、近代以前の日本における秘密工作員でした。彼らは、様々な武器や技能を用いて、戦闘、諜報活動、破壊工作、暗殺などに携わっていました。江戸時代には、忍者は政府の諜報員のようになり、大名などの行動を秘密裏に監視していました。武士による統治の終わりとともに忍者は姿を消しました。

Ninja 忍者 **VS** **Ninja in Hollywood movies** ハリウッド映画の忍者

近代以前の秘密工作員

超人的能力者（架空の存在）

Ninja を英語で説明してみよう

Q. **Did ninja have superhuman abilities like the ones in Hollywood movies?**

忍者は、ハリウッド映画の忍者のように、超人的な能力を持っていたの？

A. **Those ninja are fictional. Because ninja were mostly obscure, the images of ninja having such mysterious abilities were fostered in the Edo Period. Later, super-heroic ninja characters, who use magical skills called *ninpo*, became popular in novels, movies and manga. Hollywood movies copied them.**

その手の忍者は架空の存在だね。忍者は実態がほとんど不明だったので、不思議な能力を持っているというイメージが江戸時代に培われたんだ。その後、忍法と呼ばれる不思議な力を持つスーパーヒーローのような忍者が小説や映画やマンガで人気になったんだ。ハリウッドの映画はそれらのコピーだね。

🎎 Vocabulary 語句

agent	名 工作員		feudal lord	大名
pre-modern	形 近代以前の		reign	名 統治
engage in 〜	〜に携わる		superhuman	形 超人的な
intelligence activity	諜報活動		fictional	形 架空の
sabotage	名 破壊工作		obscure	形 実態が不明の
assassination	名 暗殺		mysterious	形 不思議な
weapon	名 武器		foster	動 〜を培う
spy	名 スパイ、諜報員		super-heroic	形 スーパーヒーローのような
monitor	動 〜を監視する		magical	形 不思議な

077

Jinrikisha
人力車

What is jinrikisha?

Jinrikisha is a human-drawn cart. After Japan modernized in the mid 19th century, it became very popular because it was faster than a palanquin and less costly than a horse-drawn cart. Although jinrikisha disappeared due to the prevalence of trains and cars, they are regaining popularity as a tourist attraction.

訳

人力車って何だろう？
人力車は人力で引く車です。日本が 19 世紀半ばに近代化を迎えた後、駕籠よりも速く、馬車よりも費用がかからないため大人気になりました。列車や自動車が普及すると人力車は姿を消しましたが、観光目玉として再び人気が出てきています。

イラストで くらべる！

Jinrikisha 人力車 **VS** **Horse-drawn cart** 馬車

Jinrikisha を英語で説明してみよう

Q. Were horse-drawn carts used in Japan, too?

日本でも馬車は使われたの？

A. Yes, but only after the mid 19th century. Before that, the use of wheels was strictly controlled to prevent possible rebellion. Roads were not paved and some huge rivers didn't have bridges for the same reason. With Japan's modernization, however, horse-drawn carts became an important means of transportation.

うん、でも 19 世紀中期以降になってからだね。それより以前は、反乱を未然に防ぐために、車輪の使用は厳しく制限されていたんだ。同じ理由で、道路は舗装されていなかったし、大きな川には橋が架かっていないものもあったんだ。でも、日本の近代化とともに、馬車は重要な交通手段になったんだよ。

🔴 Vocabulary 語句

human-drawn	形	人力で引く（人力車は英語で a rickshaw とも呼ばれるが、語源は日本語の「人力車」）
modernize	動	近代化する
palanquin	名	駕籠
horse-drawn cart		馬車
disappear	動	消える
due to ～		～のせいで

prevalence	名	普及
regain	動	～を再び得る
popularity	名	人気
tourist attraction		観光目玉
wheel	名	車輪
prevent	動	～を防ぐ
rebellion	名	反乱
be paved		舗装されている
means	名	手段、方法

078

Kofun

古墳

What is *kofun*?

Kofun are ancient burial mounds. They were built across Japan between the 3rd and 7th centuries as tombs of emperors and rulers. Among them, keyhole-shaped mounds called *zenpo-koen-fun* are unique to Japan. The biggest *kofun* in Japan is Daisenryo Kofun in Osaka Prefecture. It is 840 meters long and 654 meters wide.

古墳って何だろう？　古墳は古代の墳丘墓です。3 世紀から 7 世紀にかけて、天皇や豪族の墓として日本中に造られました。中でも、鍵穴の形をした前方後円墳と呼ばれる古墳は日本独特です。日本最大の古墳は大仙陵古墳で、長さ 840 メートル、幅 654 メートルあります。

イラストで くらべる！

Kofun 古墳 **VS** **Pyramids** ピラミッド

前方後円墳

墓

目的：諸説あり

Kofun を英語で説明してみよう

Q. ***Kofun* are similar to Pyramids in Egypt, aren't they?**

古墳って、エジプトのピラミッドに似ていない？

A. **Yes, they are similar in that both were built to show off the power of the rulers. However, although *kofun* are clearly tombs because stone burial chambers and various funerary objects have been found inside, there are many different theories about Pyramids as to their purposes. Some scholars say Pyramids were religious facilities.**

そうだね、権力者の力を誇示するために造られた点では似ているね。でも、古墳は、内部から石室やいろんな副葬品が発見されているから、確かに墓であるのに対し、ピラミッドの目的については、いろんな説があるんだよ。ピラミッドは宗教施設だったって言う学者もいるしね。

Vocabulary　語句

burial	名 埋葬	unique to ～		～に独特の
mound	名 塚、墳丘（ancient burial mound で日本の「古墳」の意味）	show off ～		～を見せつける
		burial chamber		石室（石で作られた墓室）
tomb	名 墓	funerary		形 葬儀の
keyhole-shaped	形 鍵穴の形をした	religious		形 宗教的な
		facility		名 施設

079

Koshitsu

皇室

What is *koshitsu*?

Koshitsu is Japan's Imperial Family headed by the Emperor and Empress. It is thought that the reign of the Emperor started around the 3rd century. Today, under the present constitution, the sovereignty belongs to the Japanese people and the status of the Emperor is only symbolic.

皇室って何だろう？

皇室は、天皇と皇后を筆頭とする日本の天皇家のことです。天皇による統治は3世紀頃に始まったとされます。今日、現行憲法の下では、主権は日本国民にあり、天皇の地位は象徴的でしかありません。

Koshitsu 皇室 VS Royal family ヨーロッパの王室

Koshitsu を英語で説明してみよう

Q. **Is the Imperial Family in Japan similar to the royal families in Europe?**

日本の皇室はヨーロッパの王室に似ている？

A. **Yes, it is, but because the Emperor has no political power under the present constitution, the Imperial Family tends to keep a low profile. Also, the present law stipulates that only a male descendant in the male line can become the Emperor, so Japan cannot have a female monarch.**

似ているね。でも、天皇は現行憲法下では政治権力を全く持たないので、皇室は目立つ行動を控える傾向があるね。それに現在の法律では、天皇になれる子孫は、男系の男子のみと定めているんで、女性の君主を持つことはできないんだ。

🌅 Vocabulary 語句

the Imperial Family	皇室、天皇家		belong to ～	～に属する
head	動 ～の筆頭を占める		status	名 地位
the Emperor	天皇		symbolic	形 象徴的な
the Empress	皇后		keep a low profile	目立たないようにする
reign	名 統治		stipulate	動 （法律などが）定める
the present constitution	現行憲法		descendant in the male line	男系子孫
sovereignty	名 主権		a female monarch	女性の君主

080

Katana
刀

What is katana?

Katana is a Japanese sword. It is characterized by its curved body and very sharp edge. In the Edo Period, a pair of long and short swords became a symbol of samurai. Today, katana are classified not as weapons but as art objects, and only national licensed specialists are allowed to make them.

刀って何だろう？
刀は日本刀のことです。反った刀身と極めて鋭い刃が特徴です。江戸時代には、大小の刀は武士の象徴になりました。今日では、刀は武器ではなく美術工芸品に分類されており、国家資格を持つ専門家のみが製作を許可されています。

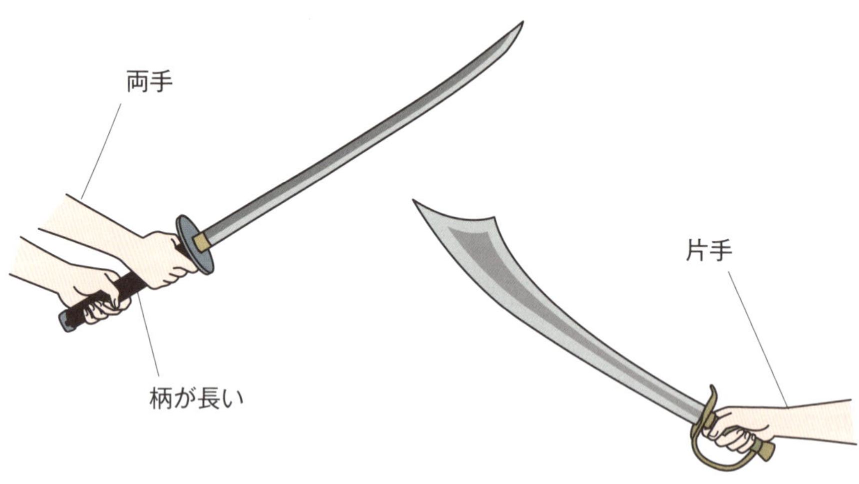

Katana を英語で説明してみよう

Q. **How is the katana different from the saber?**

刀はサーベルとどこが違うの？

A. **The saber is held in one hand, but the katana is held in both hands with the right hand forward, so the grip of the katana is made longer. Saber techniques are similar to those of fencing, while katana techniques are similar to those of kendo.**

サーベルは片手で持つけど、刀は右手を前にして両手で持つんだ。だから、刀の柄の方が長く作ってある。サーベルの技はフェンシングの技に似ているけど、刀の技は剣道の技に似ているね。

🟤Vocabulary 語句

sword	名 刀		art object	美術工芸品
curved	形 反った		national licensed	国家資格を持った
edge	名 刃		specialist	名 専門家
symbol	名 象徴		saber	名 サーベル
be classified as ～	～に分類される		grip	名 柄（刀剣などの、手で握る部分）
weapon	名 武器		be similar to ～	～に似ている

081

Meiji Ishin

明治維新

What is Meiji Ishin?

Meiji Ishin means the Meiji Restoration, a political change in mid-19th century Japan that ended the rule of samurai and restored the reign of the Emperor. It was aimed at modernizing Japan to prevent it from being colonized by Western powers. The change was successful, and in several decades, Japan joined the world powers.

明治維新って何だろう？ 明治維新は、武士の治世を終わらせ天皇の治世を復古させた、19世紀中頃の日本における政治的変革でした。明治維新は、日本が西洋列強から植民地化されるのを防ぐことを目的としていました。変革は成功し、数十年の間に日本は世界の列強の仲間入りを果たしました。

イラストで **くらべる！**

Meiji Ishin 明治維新 VS Popular revolutions 市民革命

Meiji Ishin を英語で説明してみよう

Q. Was Meiji Ishin like popular revolutions in European countries?

明治維新ってヨーロッパ諸国の市民革命に似ていた？

A. They were similar in that they toppled the authoritarian rule and established modern capitalism. However, Meiji Ishin was not a revolution because Japan's head of state had always been the Emperor and his power was literally restored. The Emperor's sovereignty was clearly declared in the Meiji Constitution promulgated in 1889.

絶対主義を打倒して近代的な資本主義を打ち立てた点においては似ているね。でも、明治維新は革命ではないんだ。日本の国家元首は常に天皇であって、文字通り天皇の権力が復古されたわけだからね。天皇の主権は、1889 年に制定された明治憲法で明確に宣言されたんだ。

Vocabulary 語句

the Meiji Restoration	明治維新（restoration は「王政復古」の意味）	topple	動 ～を打倒する
restore	動 ～を復古する	authoritarian	形 絶対主義の
reign	名 治世	establish	動 ～を打ち立てる
be aimed at ～	～を目的としている	head of state	国家元首
modernize	動 ～を近代化させる	sovereignty	名 主権、統治権
prevent ～ from ...ing	～が…するのを防ぐ	declare	動 ～を宣言する
Western powers	西洋列強（ここでの power は、「強国」の意味）	constitution	名 憲法
		promulgate	動 ～を発布する

082

Seppuku / Harakiri

切腹／腹切り

What is harakiri?

Seppuku or harakiri was the ritual of a samurai killing himself by cutting his own belly with a sword. It was practiced as a form of death punishment for samurai in the Edo Period, and was thought a more honorable way of dying than being executed.

切腹って何だろう？

切腹、あるいは腹切りは、武士が刀で自分の腹を切って自死する儀式でした。切腹は、江戸時代に、武士に対する死罪の形式として行われており、処刑されるよりも名誉のある死に方と思われていました。

Seppuku を英語で説明してみよう

Q. **Christianity sees suicide as a sin. How about in Japan?**

キリスト教では、自殺は罪とされるけど、日本ではどうなの？

A. **Shinto and Buddhism emphasize the importance of life, but they don't see death in any form from the moral point of view. Although seppuku is a thing of the past, I think it was considered a brave way of taking responsibility for wrongdoings or fulfilling social obligations.**

神道と仏教は、命の大切さを重視するけど、どんな形の死であれ、道徳的観点から死を評価することはないんだ。切腹は、もう昔の話だけど、自分の罪に対して責任を取ったり、自分の義理を果たしたりするための潔い方法だと思われていたはずだよ。

🎎 Vocabulary 語句

ritual	名 儀式	be executed		処刑される
kill oneself	自殺する、自害する（「自害」は自らを刀などで傷つけて死ぬこと）	suicide	名	自殺
		sin	名	罪
belly	名 腹	from the moral point of view		道徳的観点から
sword	名 刀	brave	形	潔い
death punishment	死罪	wrongdoing	名	罪
honorable	形 名誉のある	fulfill	動	～を果たす
die	動 死ぬ	social obligation		社会的義務、義理

083 Shogun
将軍

What is shogun?

Shogun was a title given from the Emperor to the leader of samurai in Japan's feudal era. Under this title, the shogun was allowed to establish his military government called the shogunate, or bakufu, which controlled feudal lords and their domains. The shogun's post was inherited within the shogun's family.

将軍って何だろう？
将軍は、日本の封建時代において天皇から武士の棟梁に与えられる称号でした。この称号の下で、将軍は幕府と呼ばれる自らの軍事政府を設立することができました。幕府は大名とその土地を統制しました。将軍職は将軍家の中で世襲されました。

Shogun 将軍 **VS** King 国王

Shogun を英語で説明してみよう

Q. **Was the shogun like a king in Europe?**

将軍ってヨーロッパの国王みたいなもの？

A. **Not really, because the head of state of Japan remained the Emperor all the time. Nevertheless, the Emperor's status was more like a symbol of Japan as the leader of Shinto religion. In that sense, the relations between the Emperor and the shogun were similar to those between the Pope and the king in European history.**

というわけでもないね。どの時代も日本の国家元首は天皇だったからね。とは言っても、天皇の地位は、神道という宗教の指導者として、日本の象徴という感じのときが多かったな。その意味では、天皇と将軍の関係は、西洋史のローマ教皇と国王の関係に似ていたと言えるね。

Vocabulary 語句

title	名 称号		feudal lord	大名、封建領主
the feudal era	封建時代		domain	名 領土
be allowed to do ～	～することができる		post	名 職、地位
military government	軍事政府		inherit	動 ～を世襲する
shogunate	名 幕府、将軍の地位、将軍による政治		head of state	国家元首
			nevertheless	副 とは言っても
control	動 ～を統制する		symbol	名 象徴
			the Pope	ローマ教皇

084

Hinomaru and Kimigayo
日の丸と君が代

What are Hinomaru and Kimigayo?

Hinomaru is Japan's national flag, which depicts a red circle in the center of a white background, representing the rising sun. "Kimigayo" is Japan's national anthem, whose lyrics were taken from a poem in an anthology compiled in the 10th century. Its melody was composed in the 19th century.

日の丸と君が代って何だろう？
日の丸は日本の国旗で、白地の背景の中央に赤い円が描かれており、日が昇る姿を表しています。『君が代』は日本の国歌で、その歌詞は、10 世紀に編纂された歌集の和歌から採られています。『君が代』の旋律は、19 世紀に作曲されました。

イラストで くらべる！

Kimigayo 君が代 VS The Star-Spangled Banner 星条旗

君が代は
千代に八千代に
さざれ石の
いわおとなりて
苔のむすまで

Oh, say can you see,
by the dawn's early light
What so proudly we hailed
at the twilight's last gleaming?
Whose broad stripes and bright stars,
through the perilous fight.
O'er the ramparts we watched
were so gallantly streaming?
……

Kimigayo を英語で説明してみよう

Q. **Many national anthems are about war, like "The Star-Spangled Banner" of the U.S. How about Japan's national anthem?**

多くの国歌は戦争がテーマだよね。米国の『星条旗』みたいに。日本の国歌はどう？

A. **Japan's national anthem is titled "Kimigayo", which is usually translated in English as "His Imperial Majesty's Reign", but there are different interpretations of the lyrics. In fact, there's no official translation of them. Still, it is generally believed that their theme is to wish for the everlasting reign of the Emperor.**

日本の国歌の題名は『君が代』で、"His Imperial Majesty's Reign"（天皇陛下の治世）と普通訳されるけど、この歌詞についてはいろんな解釈があるんだ。事実、公な歌詞の訳は存在しないんだよ。それでも、一般的には、歌詞のテーマは、天皇の治世が永遠に続くことを願ったものと信じられているよ。

Vocabulary 語句

national flag	国旗
depict	動 ～を描く
background	名 背景
represent	動 ～を表す
national anthem	国歌
lyrics	名 歌詞（複数形・複数扱い）
poem	名 詩（ここでは、和歌）
anthology	名 選集（ここでは、『古今和歌集』のこと）

compile	動 ～を編纂する
compose	動 ～を作曲する
"The Star-Spangled Banner"	『星条旗』（米国の国歌）
reign	名 治世
interpretation	名 解釈
theme	名 テーマ
everlasting	形 永遠に続く

085

Onsen

温泉

What is onsen?

Onsen refers to hot springs. Because Japan is a volcanic country, there are natural hot springs everywhere. Many hot spring areas have been developed as resorts, providing accommodations. Onsen resorts are usually located in mountains or on the seaside with beautiful scenery. Open-air hot spring baths called *rotenburo* are especially popular in those areas.

温泉って何だろう？　日本は火山国であるため、天然温泉がいたるところにあります。多くの温泉地域が保養地として開発され、宿泊施設を提供しています。温泉保養地は普通、美しい景色がある山の中や海岸にあります。そういった地域では、露天風呂と呼ばれる、屋外の温泉風呂が特に人気です。

イラストでくらべる！

Onsen 温泉 VS Hot spring（外国の）温泉

Onsen を英語で説明してみよう

Q. **Hot springs can be found in many other countries as well. Are Japanese onsen different from those?**

温泉は他の多くの国にもあるよね。日本の温泉は外国のものと違うの？

A. **Although the definition of onsen as to the minerals contained and the water temperatures is different according to each country, they are basically the same. The biggest difference is the way you use it. At most onsen, you cannot wear a swimsuit, and you have to clean your body before entering the bath.**

温泉の定義は、含まれるミネラルやお湯の温度など、国によって異なるけど、基本的には同じだよ。一番の違いは使い方だよ。ほとんどの温泉では水着を着てはいけないんだ。それに、お湯に入る前に、体を洗わないといけないんだよ。

🎎 Vocabulary　語句

hot spring	温泉（日本の温泉法では、25 度以上、あるいは、特定の成分を含むものと規定している）
volcanic	形 火山の
resort	名 保養地、リゾート
provide	動 ～を提供する

accommodation	名 宿泊施設（米国英語では通例～ s）
scenery	名 景色
open-air	形 屋外の
mineral	名 鉱物、ミネラル
swimsuit	名 水着

086 Teien

庭園

What is *teien*?

Teien refers to traditional Japanese-style gardens. There are two types: dry gardens and stroll gardens. Dry gardens don't use water, and instead use rocks and sand to represent mountains and waters. Stroll gardens have hills, streams, ponds and bridges, and visitors enjoy viewing changing landscapes while strolling around them.

訳 庭園って何だろう？　日本庭園は伝統的な日本式の庭園を指します。日本庭園には枯山水と回遊式庭園の２種類があります。枯山水は水を用いず、代わりに、岩や砂を使って山や海を表します。回遊式庭園は、築山、遣水、池、橋などがあり、来園者は庭園を散策しながら、変わりゆく景色を楽しみます。

イラストで くらべる！

Teien 庭園 VS European garden ヨーロッパの庭園

左右非対称

幾何学模様

Teien を英語で説明してみよう

Q. **How are Japanese gardens different from European gardens?**

日本の庭園は、ヨーロッパの庭園とどこが違うの？

A. European gardens often use geometric patterns such as straight lines, squares and circles, but Japanese gardens try to recreate natural scenes, so they look asymmetrical. Some gardens even try to incorporate the background natural scenery into the garden layout. The style is called *shakkei*, or borrowed landscape.

ヨーロッパの庭園は、よく直線、四角、円などの幾何学模様を使うけど、日本の庭園は自然の景色を再現しようとするから、左右非対称に見えるんだ。中には、背後にある自然景観を庭の設計に取り入れようとするものさえあるんだ。そのような様式は、借りた風景、つまり、借景と呼ばれるんだ。

🎎 Vocabulary 語句

dry garden	枯山水（**dry landscape garden** とも）	**landscape**	名	風景
stroll garden	回遊式庭園（**stroll-style garden** とも）	**stroll around ~**		~を歩き回る
represent	動 ~を表す	**geometric**	形	幾何学的な
waters	名 海、海域、水域（~ **s** の形で、「水域」の意味になる）	**recreate**	動	~を再現する
		asymmetrical	形	左右非対称の
hill	名 ここでは、築山	**incorporate A into B**		A を B に取り込む
stream	名 ここでは、遣水	**borrow**	動	~を借りる

087 Hanabi
花火

What is *hanabi*?

Hanabi are fireworks. Fireworks are a summer symbol in Japan. Many fireworks displays are held across the country, and people like to spend the cooler evening hours watching them. Hand-held toy *hanabi* are also popular in summer. At camping sites and the beachside, we often see children playing with them in the evening.

花火って何だろう？　花火は日本の夏の風物詩です。日本中で多くの花火大会が開かれます。日本人は涼しい夜の時間帯を、花火を見て過ごすのが好きなのです。おもちゃの手持ち花火も夏には人気です。キャンプ場や海辺などで、子供たちが夜に花火で遊んでいるのをよく見かけます。

イラストで くらべる！

Fireworks displays 花火大会  **VS** **Guy Fawkes Night ガイ・フォークス・ナイト**

Fireworks displays を英語で説明してみよう

Q. In Britain, large-scale fireworks displays are held at Guy Fawkes Night on November 5. Why in Japan are fireworks displays held in summer?

英国では、11月5日のガイ・フォークス・ナイトに大規模な花火大会が催されるよ。日本ではどうして夏に花火大会を開くの？

A. The first large-scale fireworks display in Japan was held in the Edo Period as a summer ritual to console the souls of cholera victims. It later developed into a summer custom, in which people enjoy the evening cool on the riverside while watching fireworks displays.

最初の大規模な花火大会は、江戸時代に、コレラの犠牲者を鎮魂するための夏の儀式として開かれたんだ。それが後に、川辺で花火を見ながら納涼を楽しむ夏の習慣になったんだよ。

Vocabulary 語句

firework	名 花火
symbol	名 象徴
display	名 見せ物、ショー（a firework display で花火大会の意味）
spend ~ ...ing	…しながら～を過ごす
hand-held	形 手持ちの
toy	形 おもちゃの

camping site	キャンプ場
the beachside	海辺
Guy Fawkes Night	ガイ・フォークス・ナイト（1605年に起きた Guy Fawkes によるテロ未遂事件の記念日。Fireworks Night とも）
ritual	名 儀式
console	動 ～を慰める
cholera victim	コレラの犠牲者

088

Chikatetsu

地下鉄

What is *chikatetsu*?

Chikatetsu means the subway. Japan's major cities including Tokyo, Nagoya and Osaka have extensive subway networks. Those in Tokyo are especially well-developed, with the first subway starting operation in 1927. Today, 13 subway lines are under operation in Tokyo, and more than 8.5 million passengers use them every day.

地下鉄って何だろう？　地下鉄は the subway を意味します。東京、名古屋、大阪など日本の大都市には、発達した地下鉄網があります。東京の地下鉄は、1927年に運行を開始し、特によく発達しています。今日では、東京で13の地下鉄路線が運行されており、毎日850万人以上の乗客が利用しています。

イラストで **くらべる！**

24 時間運行されている

Chikatetsu を英語で説明してみよう

Q. **The subways run 24 hours a day in New York, but they don't in Tokyo. Why?**

ニューヨークの地下鉄は 24 時間運航されているけど、日本は違うよね。どうして？

A. **The New York City Subways were designed to operate 24 hours a day from the beginning, having extra rails for maintenance. Tokyo's subways need to stop the service during the night for maintenance. The subway companies, however, are now thinking about extending operation hours in the future.**

ニューヨーク市地下鉄は、最初から 24 時間運航できるように設計されていて、保守作業用の余分なレールが装備されているんだ。でも、地下鉄会社は今、将来的に運行時間を長くすることを検討中なんだ。

🎎 Vocabulary 語句

major city	大都市		**from the beginning**	最初から
extensive	形 範囲の広い、発達した		**maintenance**	名 保守作業
well-developed	形 よく発達した		**extend**	動 ～を延長する
operation	名 運行		**operation hours**	運行時間
passenger	名 乗客			
be designed to do ～	～するように設計されている			

089

Ekiben

駅弁

What is ekiben?

Ekiben are packed meals sold at train stations. "Eki" means a train station and "ben" means bento, a packed meal. Enjoying an ekiben on board is a great pleasure for many train travelers. They are so popular that department stores often have an ekiben fair, selling ekiben from across the country.

駅弁って何だろう？ 　駅弁は鉄道駅で売られている箱詰めの食事です。Eki は鉄道駅の意味、ben は弁当、つまり箱詰めの食事のことです。乗車中に駅弁を食すのは、多くの鉄道旅行者にとって大きな楽しみです。駅弁はとても人気で、デパートでは、よく日本各地の駅弁を売る駅弁フェアが行われています。

イラストで **くらべる！**

Ekiben 駅弁 **VS** Train meals 列車での食事

地域の特産物

箱詰めの食事

CandyBox Images/PIXTA（ピクスタ）

サンドイッチ

Ekiben を英語で説明してみよう

Q. **Train meals are available in other cultures, too. What is unique about ekiben?**

列車での食事って他の文化圏にもあるよね。駅弁は何が独特なの？

A. **Ekiben are different according to the region, with each featuring the region's local delicacies and culture. Some are available only in a particular season. The containers are also unique. Some are shaped like the delicacies used such as a crab, and others use the region's famous handicrafts such as Arita ware.**

駅弁は地域によって異なっていて、それぞれが、その地域の特産物や文化を目玉にしているんだ。中には、特定の季節にしか買えないものもあるしね。容器がまた独特なんだ。カニとか、使用している特産物の形をしているものもあれば、有田焼とか、地元の有名な工芸品を用いているものもあるね。

Vocabulary 語句

packed meal	箱詰めの食事		from across the country	国中からの
on board	乗車中に		feature	動 ～を目玉にする
pleasure	名 楽しみ、喜び		delicacy	名 ごちそう
department store	デパート		container	名 容器
fair	名 フェア、展示（販売）会		handicraft	名 工芸品

223

090

Tokyo

東京

What is Tokyo?

Tokyo is the capital of Japan. Tokyo is Japan's political and economic center, and is home to over 13 million people. In the old days, Tokyo was called Edo. It flourished as the seat of the Tokugawa shogunate. Therefore, Tokyo has many historical sites along with modern high-rise buildings.

東京って何だろう？　東京は日本の首都です。東京は日本の政治・経済の中心で、1300万人以上の人が住んでいます。昔、東京は江戸と呼ばれました。江戸は、江戸幕府が置かれた地として栄えました。そのため東京には、現代的な高層ビルと並んで、数多くの史跡があります。

イラストでくらべる！

Tokyo 東京 VS New York ニューヨーク

高層ビル

道路が込み入っている

碁盤目状に設計された

Tokyo を英語で説明してみよう

Q. **Some people say Tokyo is like New York. Do you agree?**

東京はニューヨークみたいと言う人がいるけど、そう思う？

A. **Yes, I partly agree. They both have high-rises, commercial districts, parks, and huge crowds of people everywhere, but whereas New York was planned on a grid, Tokyo developed without much city planning, so the roads are quite complicated. Also, New York is culturally very diverse, but Tokyo retains many traditional Japanese cultural aspects.**

ある程度そう思うね。どちらも、いたるところに高層ビル、商業地区、公園、人混みがあるからね。でも、ニューヨークが碁盤目状に設計されたのに対し、東京は都市計画があまりない状態で発達したから、道路がとても込み入っているね。それに、ニューヨークは文化的にとても多様だけど、東京は伝統的な日本文化の側面を多く残しているな。

🎎 Vocabulary 語句

capital	名 首都	along with ～	～と並んで
be home to ～	～が住んでいる	high-rise building	高層ビル、摩天楼
flourish	動 栄える	commercial district	商業地区
seat	名 所在地	be planned on a grid	碁盤目状に設計される
shogunate	名 幕府、将軍の地位、将軍による政治	city planning	都市計画
historical site	史跡		

091

Kyoto

京都

What is Kyoto?

Kyoto was Japan's capital for more than 1,000 years from the late 8th century to the mid 19th century. Located in the western part of Honshu, Kyoto had long been Japan's political and cultural center where the Emperor lived. Kyoto has numerous historical sites, many of which are placed on the World Heritage List.

京都って何だろう？
京都は 8 世紀末から 19 世紀半ばまで、千年近く日本の首都でした。本州の西部に位置している京都は、天皇が住む地として長い間、日本の政治と文化の中心でした。京都には無数の史跡があり、その多くが世界遺産リストに掲載されています。

イラストで くらべる！

Kyoto 京都　VS　London ロンドン

文化はとても日本的

文化が多様化

Kyoto を英語で説明してみよう

Q. **I think Kyoto has a lot in common with London. What do you think?**

京都はロンドンと多くの共通点があると思うけど、どう？

A. I agree. Kyoto is an ancient capital, where the Imperial family lived, while London is the UK's capital, where the Royal family lives. Both are rich in tradition and culture, having many historical buildings. One difference is that London's culture is very diverse, whereas Kyoto's culture is distinctively Japanese.

同感だね。京都は日本の古都で、皇室が住んでおられたし、ロンドンは英国の首都で、王室が住んでおられるよね。どちらも豊かな伝統と文化があって、多くの伝統的建造物がある。1つ違いがあるとすれば、ロンドンの文化がとても多様化している一方で、京都の文化は実に日本的というところかな。

🎎 Vocabulary 語句

capital	名 首都	be placed on the World Heritage List	世界遺産リストに掲載されている
long	副 長い間（副詞の用法）	have a lot in common with ~	~と多くの共通点がある
political and cultural center	政治と文化の中心	diverse	形 多様化した
numerous	形 無数の	distinctively	副 明確に
historical site	史跡	Japanese	形 日本的な

092

Tokyo Tower

東京タワー

What is Tokyo Tower?

Tokyo Tower is a broadcast tower located in the center of Tokyo. It was completed in 1958, and was the world's tallest self-supporting steel structure then with the height of 333 meters. It has two observation decks, where various events are held throughout the year. Tokyo Tower attracts around three million visitors annually.

東京タワーって何だろう？ 東京タワーは東京の中心に位置する電波塔です。東京タワーが完成したのは 1958 年で、高さ 333 メートルあり当時、世界で最も高い自立鉄塔でした。東京タワーには 2 つの展望台があり、1 年中様々なイベントが開かれています。東京タワーを訪れる人は年間約 300 万人に上ります。

イラストで **くらべる！**

高さ：**333** m

高さ：**324** m

Tokyo Tower を英語で説明してみよう

Q. **Tokyo Tower resembles the Eiffel Tower in Paris, doesn't it?**

東京タワーはパリのエッフェル塔に似ていない？

A. **Well, it does, because both are symbolic landmarks of their respective capital cities. The biggest difference is the purpose of the tower. TV broadcasting started in Japan in 1953, and Tokyo Tower was built to send TV and radio signals around the Kanto Area centering Tokyo.**

そうだね、どちらも、それぞれの首都を象徴する名所だしね。一番違う点は、塔の目的だね。日本ではテレビ放送が 1953 年に始まったんだけど、東京タワーは、東京を中心とした関東一円にテレビ放送やラジオ放送の電波を送るために建てられたんだ。

🟥 Vocabulary　語句

broadcast tower	電波塔	annually	副 毎年
complete	動 ～を完成する	the Eiffel Tower	エッフェル塔（1889 年のパリ万博の目玉として建設、その後、電波塔としても使用されている）
self-supporting steel structure	自立鉄塔		
height	名 高さ	symbolic	形 象徴的な
observation deck	展望台	landmark	名 目印になる建物、名所
attract	動 ～を引き付ける、～の人たちが訪れる	purpose	名 目的

229

093 Tottori Sakyu
鳥取砂丘

What is Tottori Sakyu?

Tottori Sakyu are sand dunes located in Tottori Prefecture in western Honshu. They are the largest sand dunes in Japan, stretching 16 km east to west and 2.4 km north to south. Tottori Sakyu is designated as a natural monument and is part of the Sanin Kaigan National Park.

鳥取砂丘って何だろう？

鳥取砂丘は、本州西部の鳥取県にある砂丘です。鳥取砂丘は、東西16キロメートル、南北2.4キロメートルに及ぶ日本最大の砂丘です。鳥取砂丘は天然記念物に指定されており、山陰海岸国立公園の一部になっています。

イラストで くらべる！

Tottori Sakyu を英語で説明してみよう

Q. **Its photo reminds me of the Sahara. How is it different from a desert?**

写真を見たら、サハラ砂漠が頭に浮かんだよ。砂漠とはどう違うの？

A. **Deserts like the Sahara are found in the tropical or the sub-tropical areas. They are very dry, so few plants can grow. However, most parts of Japan have a humid mild temperate climate, so Tottori Sakyu has a lot of rain. Plants do grow there, though they are periodically removed for better views.**

サハラ砂漠のような砂漠は、熱帯地域か亜熱帯地域にあるんだ。そういった砂漠はとても乾燥してるから植物がほとんど生えないんだよ。ところが、日本は大部分が温暖湿潤気候に属しているから、鳥取砂丘では雨が多く降るんだ。実際、植物も生えるんだ。景観を良くするために定期的に取り除かれているけれどね。

🔴 Vocabulary 語句

sand dune	砂丘	tropical	形 熱帯の
stretch	動 広がる、延びる	sub-tropical	形 亜熱帯の
be designated as ～	～に指定される	a humid mild temperate climate	温暖湿潤気候
natural monument	天然記念物		
part of ～	～の一部	periodically	副 定期的に
desert	名 砂漠	remove	動 ～を取り除く

094

The Japanese Alps
日本アルプス

What are the Japanese Alps?

The Japanese Alps are a series of mountain ranges located in the middle part of Honshu Island. They consist of the Hida Mountains, the Kiso Mountains and the Akaishi Mountains. Many mountains in the Japanese Alps are over 3,000 meters high, and are popular with mountain climbers from home and abroad.

日本アルプスって何だろう？
日本アルプスは、本州中央に位置する一連の山岳地帯で、飛騨山脈、木曽山脈、赤石山脈からなっています。日本アルプスの多くの山は、標高 3,000 メートル以上あり、国内外からの登山客に人気です。

イラストで **くらべる！**

The Japanese Alps を英語で説明してみよう

Q. **Why are they called the Japanese Alps?**

どうして、日本アルプスって呼ばれているの？

A. A British archaeologist named William Gowland, who introduced Western mountain climbing into Japan, coined the term in the late 19th century. Later, an English missionary named Walter Weston climbed part of the Japanese Alps and wrote about it in his book, making the name world-famous.

日本に西洋登山をもたらした、ウィリアム・ゴウランドという名のイギリス人考古学者が 19 世紀末にその名を付けたんだ。のちに、ウォルター・ウェストンという名のイギリス人宣教師が日本アルプスの一部に登って、そのことを本に書いたので、世界的にその名が知られることになったんだよ。

Vocabulary 語句

the Japanese Alps	日本アルプス（最初は飛騨山脈のみを意味したが、後に、木曽山脈と赤石山脈を合わせてこのように呼ぶようになった）	mountain climber	登山客、登山家
		from home and abroad	国内外の
a series of ～	一連の～	archaeologist	名 考古学者
		coin	動 （言葉を）作り出す
mountain range	山岳地帯、山脈	missionary	名 宣教師

095

Setonaikai

瀬戸内海

What is Setonaikai?

Setonaikai, or the Seto Inland Sea, is located between the western part of Honshu Island and Shikoku Island. The waters on Setonaikai are calm, and are dotted with numerous small islands. As one of the most beautiful areas in Japan, the Seto Inland Sea is designated as a national park.

瀬戸内海って何だろう？
瀬戸内海は、本州西部と四国の間に位置しています。瀬戸内海の海域は穏やかで、無数の小さな島が点在しています。日本で最も美しい地域の1つとして、瀬戸内海は国立公園に指定されています。

イラストで **くらべる！**

Setonaikai を英語で説明してみよう

Q. **Do you think Setonaikai is similar to the Mediterranean?**

瀬戸内海は地中海に似ていると思う？

A. Yes, I do. They are geographically similar in that both are surrounded by mountains, so the roads leading to ports are steep, narrow and winding. Also, since ancient times, both have been used for transporting people, goods and information, making the areas culturally rich.

そう思うね。地中海と瀬戸内海は地理的に似ていて、どちらも山に囲まれているから、港までの道は、坂が急で細くて曲がりくねっているよね。それに古代から、どちらも人やものや情報を運ぶのに使われてきたから文化的に豊かだしね。

🎎 Vocabulary 語句

waters	名 海域		designate A as B	A を B に指定する
calm	形 穏やかな		national park	国立公園
be dotted with ～	～が点在する		the Mediterranean	地中海
numerous	形 無数の		geographically	副 地理的に

235

096

Samurai

侍

What are samurai?

Samurai were Japanese warriors in the pre-modern days. They originally served aristocrats as security guards, but at the end of the 12th century, they came into power, establishing their military government called the *bakufu*. The rule of samurai ended in the mid 19th century when Japan modernized.

侍って何だろう？
侍は、近代以前の日本の武人です。もともと、警護兵として貴族に仕えていましたが、12世紀末に政権の座に就き、幕府と呼ばれる自らの軍事政権を確立しました。侍の治世は、日本が近代化を迎える19世紀半ばに終わりました。

イラストで くらべる！

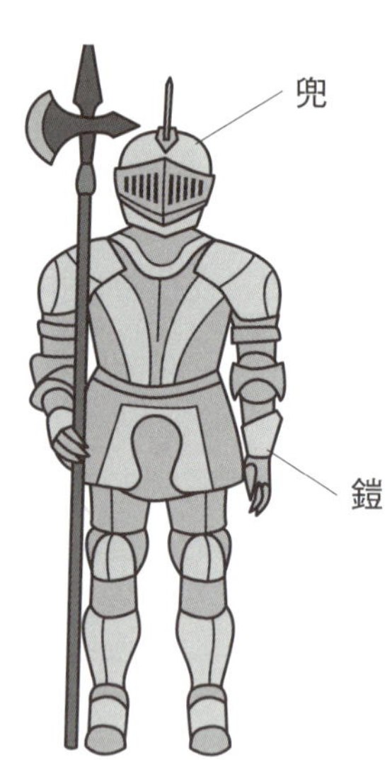

Samurai を英語で説明してみよう

Q. Are samurai similar to knights in European countries of the Middle Ages?

侍は、中世のヨーロッパ諸国にいた騎士と似ている？

A. Yes, they are. They both highly valued loyalty, courage and honor. But samurai emphasized stricter moral obligations. That's why even today, people who have strong aspirations and self-discipline are often called samurai, as in the case of SAMURAI JAPAN, the Japanese international baseball team.

うん、似ているね。どちらも、忠誠、勇気、名誉をとても重んじるからね。でも侍は、より厳しい道徳的義務を重視していたんだ。だから今日でも、志が高く、自制心が強い人たちはしばしば侍と呼ばれるんだ。ちょうど日本野球代表、「侍ジャパン」のようにね。

Vocabulary 語句

warrior	名 武人、武士		loyalty	名 忠誠
serve ～	動 ～に仕える		courage	名 勇気
aristocrat	名 貴族		honor	名 名誉
security guard	警護兵		emphasize	動 ～を強調する、～を重視する
come into power	権力の座に就く		strict	形 厳しい
military government	軍事政権		moral obligation	道徳的義務
modernize	動 近代化する		aspiration	名 大志
value	動 ～を重んじる		self-discipline	名 自制心

Q. **What weapons did samurai mainly use?**

武士が主に使っていた武器は？

A. Samurai carried swords, but on the battlefields, they mainly used spears or bows and arrows. Guns were also used after they were introduced to Japan in the 16th century. In the Edo Period, carrying two swords became a symbol of samurai, but they rarely used them in combat except in the late Edo Period, when incidents of assassination of political enemies frequently occurred.

武士は刀を持っていたけど、戦場では主に槍や弓矢を使っていたんだ。16世紀に鉄砲が日本に伝来した後は、鉄砲も使われるようになったけどね。江戸時代には2本の刀を差すのが武士の象徴になったけど、政敵の暗殺事件が頻繁に起きた江戸末期を除いて、刀を戦いで使うことはほとんどなかったね。

Q. **Do samurai still exist?**

サムライって今でもいるの？

A. No, they don't. With the modernization of Japan in the mid 19th century, samurai class disappeared altogether. Still, samurai's spirit remained the basis of Japanese moral values not only in modern martial arts such as judo and kendo, but also in business.

いや、いないよ。19世紀半ばの日本の近代化とともに、武士階級は完全に消え去ったんだ。それでも、武士の精神は今でも、柔道や剣道といった近代的な武道だけでなく、ビジネスにおいても、日本人の道徳的価値観の基盤になっているよ。

Q. **Samurai wore a topknot. Why?**

武士って髪をトップノットにしていたよね。どうして？

A. **That hairstyle is called *chon-mage*. They shaved the front of their head, and tied the remaining hair in a knot and placed it on the shaved part. When they wore a helmet, their head became very sweaty. That's why they shaved their heads.**

あの髪型は丁髷と呼ばれるんだ。前頭部を剃って、残った髪の毛をくくって、剃った部分にのせているんだ。武士が兜を着けると、頭が汗で蒸れてしまうんだ。それで前頭部を剃っていたんだよ。

 Vocabulary　語句

battlefield	名 戦場		altogether	副 完全に
spear	名 槍		basis	名 基盤
bows and arrows	弓矢		moral value	道徳的価値観
assassination	名 暗殺		shave	動 〜を剃る
enemy	名 敵		tie	動 〜をくくる
modernization	名 近代化		helmet	名 ここでは、兜
disappear	動 消える		sweaty	形 汗をかく、汗で蒸れる

097

Shiro

城

What is *shiro*?

Shiro refers to Japanese castles. The donjon is built on massive stone walls surrounded by moats. Many *shiro* were lost in the process of Japan's modernization, but some cities have preserved original castles built around the 16th century, while others rebuilt them as tourist attractions after World War II.

城って何だろう？ 城は日本の城郭を指します。天守閣は、周囲を堀で囲まれた重厚な石垣の上に建てられています。日本の近代化の過程で多くの城が失われましたが、16世紀前後に建てられた当時の城を保存してきた都市もありますし、戦後になって観光目玉として城を再建した都市もあります。

イラストで くらべる！

Shiro 城 **VS** European castle ヨーロッパの城郭

木造

石造

Shiro を英語で説明してみよう

Q. **Most European castles are made of stone, but why are Japanese castle towers made of wood?**

ヨーロッパの城郭のほとんどは石造だけど、どうして日本の城楼は木造なの？

A. **One clear reason is that in Japan, due to its hot and humid climate in summer, it's impossible to live in a stone structure. Besides, when most castles were built, there were no cannons in Japan that could reach the towers from the outside of the moats.**

1つの明確な理由は、日本では、夏の蒸し暑い気候のために、石造の建物に住むのは不可能だということだね。加えて、ほとんどの城が建造された時代には、堀の外側から城楼に届くような大砲が日本にはなかったしね。

🎎Vocabulary 語句

donjon	名 天守閣、本丸	**rebuild**	動 ～を再建する
massive	形 重厚な	**tourist attraction**	観光目玉
stone wall	石垣	**castle towers**	城楼（天守閣や櫓のこと）
moat	名 堀	**humid**	形 湿度の高い
modernization	名 近代化	**cannon**	名 大砲
preserve	動 保存する		

A. Yes, they were. Some of the oldest castles in Japan were built in Kyushu to defend against overseas invasion. Around the 8th and 9th centuries, the Imperial Court expanded its reign into the northern part of Japan, and castles were built there as its military bases. In the Middle Ages, many mountaintop castles were built by samurai, and in the Warring States Period of the late 16th century, they evolved into hill castles and flatland castles, which we recognize as *shiro* today.

あったよ。日本で最古クラスの城は、海外からの侵略から防衛するために九州に築かれたんだ。8～9世紀頃には、朝廷が日本の北部へと統治権を拡大して、そこに軍事基地として城を築いたよ。中世には、武士が数多くの山城を築いたけど、16世紀の戦国時代には、今日われわれが城と認識する、平山城や平城に進化していったんだ。

Q. **Please tell me about the history of *shiro* after the 16th century.**

16 世紀以降の城の歴史を教えて。

A. There were about 3,000 *shiro* in Japan in the late 16th century, but the Tokugawa Shogunate allowed feudal lords to own only one castle, reducing the number to about 170. Because there was virtually no war, the role of castles changed from being a military fortress to a symbol of feudal lords. In the Meiji Period, many were demolished, and during World War II, many remaining *shiro* were destroyed by air raids. As a result, today, only twelve *shiro* remain from the feudal eras.

16 世紀末には、およそ 3,000 の城が日本にあったけど、江戸幕府は大名が城を 1 つだけしか持つことを許さなかったから、城の数も約 170 に減ってしまったんだ。戦争はほとんどなかったから、城の役割も、軍事要塞から大名の象徴へと変わっていったんだ。明治時代には多くが解体され、第二次世界大戦時には残った多くの城が空爆で破壊されたな。その結果、今日、封建時代から残っている城は 12 件だけだね。

🟥 Vocabulary　語句

defend against ～	～から防衛する		recognize A as B	A を B と認識する
invasion	名 侵略		feudal lord	大名
reign	名 統治		virtually	副 ほとんど
military base	軍事基地		military fortress	軍事要塞
mountaintop castle	山城		symbol	名 象徴
evolve into ～	～へと進化する		demolish	動 ～を解体する
hill castle	平山城		destroy	動 ～を破壊する
flatland castle	平城		air raid	空爆

098

Ryokan
旅館

What is ryokan?

Ryokan are traditional Japanese-style inns. They have tatami rooms and large communal baths, often outdoor hot spring baths. They offer futon for bedding and Japanese meals. Ryokan are usually located in sightseeing spots and hot spring resorts. Ryokan are a good choice for foreign visitors who want to experience traditional Japanese lifestyles.

旅館って何だろう？　旅館は伝統的な日本式の宿です。旅館には畳部屋と大浴場があり、しばしば温泉の露天風呂があったりします。旅館では寝具に布団を用意し、食事は和食になります。旅館は通常、観光地や温泉郷などにあります。旅館は、伝統的な日本の生活様式を経験したい外国人客にはピッタリです。

イラストで **くらべる！**

Ryokan 旅館 **VS** **Hotel** ホテル

畳部屋

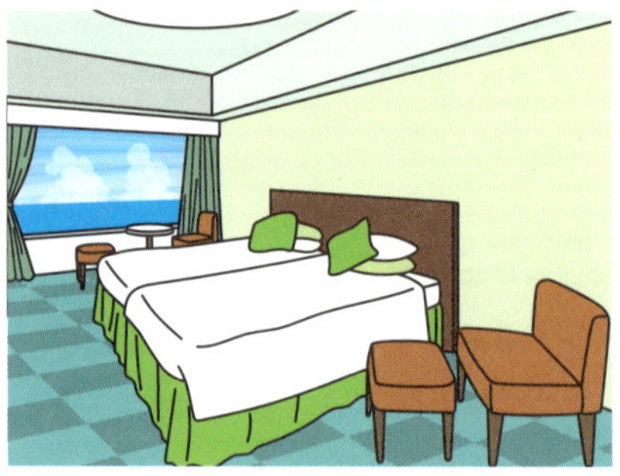

洋室

Ryokan を英語で説明してみよう

Q. How are ryokan services different from those at hotels?

旅館のサービスは、ホテルとどう違う？

A. Ryokan services are based on traditional Japanese culture, so you might feel a bit strange at first. For example, you have to be naked in a communal bath, and ryokan staff might enter your room to prepare futon while you're away. Also, the dinner menu is mostly fixed.

旅館のサービスは伝統的な日本文化に基づいているから、最初はちょっと違和感があるかもね。例えば、共同浴場では、裸にならないといけないし、不在の間に、旅館のスタッフが布団を敷きに部屋に入るかもしれないしね。それに、夕食のメニューもある程度決まってるんだ。

Vocabulary 語句

inn	名 宿	hot spring resort	温泉郷
communal bath	共同浴場	choice	名 選択
hot spring bath	温泉風呂	experience	動 〜を経験する
bedding	名 寝具	feel strange	違和感がある
meal	名 食事（1回分の食事を言う）	naked	形 裸の
sightseeing spot	観光地	fixed	形 固定されている

Q. **Please tell me more about large communal baths at ryokan.**

旅館の広い共同浴場のことをもう少し教えて。

A. **They are separated for men and women. There is a changing room at the entrance to the bath area. Guests take off their clothes and place them in a basket or on a shelf. Inside the bath area, there are one or more large baths and a separate section for washing.**

共同浴場は男女に分かれている。浴場の入口に着替え場があって、そこで客は服を脱いで籠に入れるか棚の上に置くんだ。浴場内部には、いくつかの大きな浴槽と、身体を洗うための場所が用意してあるよ。

Q. **How do you use the communal baths?**

共同浴場の使い方は？

A. **There are some rules. Wash your body at the washing section before you go into the bath. The towel you used for washing should never go into the bathwater. You might see some Japanese people put their towel on their heads while they are in the bath. Wipe your body lightly with your hand towel before you return to the changing room.**

いくつかルールがあるんだ。お湯に入る前に、洗い場で体を洗うんだ。体を洗うときに使ったタオルは浴槽のお湯に浸けないように。お湯に浸かっている間、タオルを頭にのせている日本人を見かけるはずだよ。着替え場に戻る前に、自分のハンドタオルで軽く体を拭いておくこと。

Q. How are *minshuku* different from ryokan?

民宿は旅館とどう違う？

A. Ryokan are comparable to hotels, while *minshuku* are family-run inns. They are ordinary private houses remodeled to accommodate visitors, so their rates are usually lower than those of ryokan. Although the services may be limited at *minshuku*, they are popular for their homely atmosphere.

旅館はホテルに匹敵する存在だけど、民宿は家族経営の宿なんだ。民宿は客を泊めるために改装された一般の個人住宅なんだ。だから、値段も普通、旅館よりも安い。民宿ではサービスも限られているかもしれないけど、家庭的な雰囲気があるから人気だよ。

Vocabulary 語句

changing room	着替え室
wipe	動 ～を拭く
comparable to ～	～に匹敵する
family-run	形 家族経営の
remodel	動 ～を改装する
accommodate	動 ～を泊める、～を収容する
homely	形 家庭的な（米では homey とも）

099 Shinkansen

新幹線

What is shinkansen?

Shinkansen refers to Japan's high-speed railway system, which started its operation between Tokyo and Osaka just before the opening of the 1964 Tokyo Olympic Games. Today, the shinkansen connects major cities in Hokkaido, Honshu and Kyushu. The shinkansen has a very high reputation for its safety and punctuality.

新幹線って何だろう？

新幹線は日本の高速鉄道網を指します。1964 年の東京オリンピック開幕直前に、東京・大阪間で運行を開始しました。今日、新幹線は北海道、本州、九州の主要都市を結んでいます。新幹線は、安全性と時間の正確さで評判が高いです。

Shinkansen 新幹線　VS　TGV フランスの TGV

モリゾ／PIXTA（ピクスタ）

Shinkansen を英語で説明してみよう

Q. **How is the shinkansen different from TGV in France?**

新幹線はフランスの TGV とどう違う？

A. **Each shinkansen carriage has motors, so power is decentralized in the shinkansen system, whereas with the TGV, only the front and rear cars have motors. One merit of the former system enables quicker acceleration and deceleration, so it's more suitable for the shinkansen, which runs on a tighter timetable.**

新幹線の車両はそれぞれが動力を持っているから、新幹線システムの場合、動力が分散化されているんだけど、TGV では先頭車両と最後尾車両のみが動力を持っているんだ。前者の1つの利点は、加速と減速が速くできることで、より過密なスケジュールで運行している新幹線には向いていると言えるね。

Vocabulary 語句

high-speed railway system	高速鉄道網
operation	名 運行
connect	動 ～を結ぶ
reputation	名 評判
safety	名 安全性
punctuality	名 時間の正確さ
TGV	フランスの高速鉄道
decentralized	形 分散化して（新幹線は動力分散方式で、各車両が動力を持っている一方、**TGV** は動力集中方式、または、**push-pull system** と呼ばれ、先頭車両と最後尾車両が動力を持っている）
acceleration	名 加速（⇔減速：**deceleration**）
tight	形 （スケジュールなどが）過密な
timetable	名 時刻表

Q. **How is the shinkansen different from the conventional railways?**

新幹線は在来線とどう違う？

A. **The shinkansen's track gauge is wider. Japan's most conventional lines use the narrow gauge of 1,067mm. When railways were first built in Japan, smaller trains using the narrow gauge were introduced to contain the cost. But after World War II, it became necessary to increase the speed and capacity of railway transportation by introducing larger and faster trains using the standard gauge of 1,435mm. That's why the shinkansen was built.**

新幹線の軌間は広いんだ。日本のほとんどの在来線は1,067 ミリの狭軌を使っているんだ。鉄道が日本で最初に敷設されたとき、コストを抑えるために、狭軌を使う小型の列車が導入されたんだ。だけど、第二次世界大戦後、1,435 ミリの標準軌を使う、より大きくて速い列車を導入することで、鉄道輸送の速度と運搬能力を高める必要が出てきたんだ。だから新幹線が建設されたんだよ。

Q. What is the mini-shinkansen?

ミニ新幹線って何？

A. The mini-shinkansen uses the conventional lines that have been converted to either regular gauge tracks or dual gauge tracks having an extra rail outside the existing narrow gauge tracks. This system enables direct connection between the conventional lines and the regular shinkansen lines. Currently, there are two mini-shinkansen lines: the Yamagata Shinkansen and the Akita Shinkansen. Because their curves are sharper and tunnels are narrower, the maximum speed is set lower and train bodies are made smaller. That's why they are called the mini-shinkansen.

ミニ新幹線は、標準軌道、あるいは、既存の狭軌の外側にもう１本レールを引いた三線軌道に改造された在来線を使うんだ。この方式で、在来線とフル規格の新幹線を直接結ぶことができるんだ。現在、山形新幹線と秋田新幹線の２つのミニ新幹線があるよ。これらの路線のカーブは急だし、トンネルも狭いから、最高速度は低めに定められてて、車体も小さく作られている。だから、ミニ新幹線と呼ばれるんだ。

Vocabulary 語句

conventional line	在来線		capacity	名 能力
track gauge	軌間（線路の幅）		convert	動 ～を改造する
narrow gauge	狭軌		existing	形 既存の
contain	動 ～を抑える		maximum speed	最高速度

251

Mount Fuji

富士山

What is Mount Fuji?

Mount Fuji is the highest mountain in Japan at 3,776 meters. It is located in the central part of Honshu Island, about 100 kilometers west of Tokyo. Mount Fuji is an active volcano, which last erupted in 1707. For its beautiful cone shape, Mount Fuji has been a frequent subject of Japanese art.

富士山って何だろう？　富士山は標高 3,776 メートルの日本で最も高い山です。富士山は本州の中央、東京の約 100 キロメートル西に位置しています。富士山は活火山で、前回噴火したのは 1707 年のことでした。その美しい円錐形の姿のために、日本の芸術の主題として頻繁に取り上げられてきました。

イラストで **くらべる！**

高さ：**3,776** m

kamchatka/PIXTA（ピクスタ）

高さ：**2,917** m

Mount Fuji を英語で説明してみよう

Q. Some mountains in the world are associated with religions, like Mount Olympus in Greek mythology and Mount Sinai in Judaism. How about Japanese mountains?

世界の山には、ギリシャ神話のオリンポス山やユダヤ教のシナイ山のように、宗教に結びついているものがあるよね。日本の山はどうなの？

A. In Japan, too, mountains have long been an object of worship, so even today many Japanese climb mountains as part of religious activities. Climbing Mount Fuji became especially popular in the Edo Period. There are many religious structures in the area, many of which are registered as World Heritage Sites.

日本でも、山は昔から信仰の対象だったんで、今でも多くの日本人が宗教活動の一環として登山をしているよ。富士登山は特に江戸時代に人気になったんだ。富士地域には多くの宗教関連の建物があって、その多くが世界遺産に登録されているよ。

🎎 Vocabulary 語句

active volcano	活火山	subject	名	主題
last	副 前回（副詞用法）	climb	動	～に登る
erupt	動 噴火する	structure	名	建物
cone shape	円錐形の形	register A as B		A を B として登録する

Q. **Are ordinary people allowed to climb Mount Fuji?**

普通の人でも富士山に登っていいの？

A. **Yes, they are, but it is open to the public only during summer for safety. Also, the weather changes quickly at the upper part of the mountain, so it is strongly recommended that you are escorted by experienced guides. Cars are allowed up to the fifth station at altitudes around 2,000 meters. If you want to see the sunrise from the top, you need to stay overnight at a lodge at the eighth station, and proceed to the summit early the following morning.**

うん、いいよ。ただし、富士山が一般の人たちに開かれているのは、安全のために夏だけだよ。それに、山の上部では天候が急に変わるから、経験を積んだガイドに同伴してもらうことを強くお勧めするよ。自動車でいけるのは、標高 2,000 メートルあたりの五合目まで。頂上から日の出を見たい場合は、八合目の宿で1泊して、翌日早朝に頂上を目指す必要があるよ。

What are some representative works of art depicting Mount Fuji?

富士山を描いた代表的な美術作品って何？

A. I think the most famous pieces are the series of the 36 Views of Mount Fuji created by the ukiyo-e artist, Katsushika Hokusai, in the early 19th century. The series became so popular that ten more pieces were added, so it consists of 46 ukiyo-e prints. In its creation, Hokusai used deep perspective and dynamic compositions. The series exerted a great influence on European art, especially impressionism in the 19th century, creating the Japonism boom.

最も有名な作品は、19 世紀初期に浮世絵師の葛飾北斎によって製作された『富嶽三十六景』のシリーズだと思うよ。このシリーズはとても人気になったから 10 図が加えられたんで、46 図の浮世絵からなっている。その作成において、北斎は深い遠近法や大胆な構図を使っているんだ。このシリーズは西洋美術、特に 19 世紀の印象派に大きな影響を与えて、ジャポニズムのブームを引き起こしたんだよ。

第四章　歴史・観光

🎎 Vocabulary 語句

escort	動 ～に同伴する	composition	名 構図
experienced	形 経験を積んだ	exert influence on ～	～に影響を与える
altitude	名 標高	impressionism	名 印象主義
proceed to ～	～に向かう	Japonism	名 ジャポニズム（19 世紀後半にヨーロッパで見られた日本趣味）
summit	名 頂上		
perspective	名 遠近法		
dynamic	形 大胆な		

Mount Fuji か Mount Huzi か？

　現在、小学校 3 年の国語授業の一環としてローマ字が扱われています。そこで教えられるローマ字は、英語を使う人やパソコンでローマ字入力をしている人にはあまり馴染みのない「訓令式」と呼ばれるもので、1937 年に日本政府によって正式に定められたものです。それに従うと、富士山は、Mount Huzi になります。

　一方、Fuji という表記はヘボン式と呼ばれ、米国の宣教師 James Curtis Hepburn が発明した、アルファベットによる日本語の表記法に基づきます。Hepburn の発音は日本語のヘボンに近く、ヘボン式と呼ばれるようになりました。英語の公文書における日本語の表記やパスポート上の氏名、および、駅名標や道路標識などに用いられています。

　もともと、ヘボン式は、英語の話者にとって発音しやすいように、日本語の発音にアルファベットを充てたものなので、英語圏の人には使いやすいのですが、日本語の 50 音で考えた場合、ハ行の ha, hi, fu（訓令式では hu）, he, ho や、ザ行の za, ji（訓令式では zi）, zu, ze, zo のように、fu と ji において、不規則性が生じるため、日本人にとってより論理的である表記法として訓令式が考案されました。

　アルファベットを用いる言語は英語だけではありませんし、ヘボン式で表記された chi（チ、訓令式では ti）なども必ずしも「チ」と発音してくれる言語ばかりではありません。そこで、発信する側、つまり、日本人の観点に立って、規則的なローマ字の用い方を提示するのが訓令式です。状況によってどちらを使うべきか意見が分かれるところですが、外国語で日本文化を紹介する機会がある人は、両者の区別を知っておいたほうがよさそうです。

その他
Others

101

Nengajo

年賀状

What is *nengajo*?

Nengajo are New Year's greeting postcards that are sent to relatives, friends and business acquaintances. People write greeting messages and often add some photos and pictures. Pictures of the Chinese zodiac sign of the New Year are especially popular. They use special postcards that contain lottery numbers for various prizes.

年賀状って何だろう？

年賀状は、親戚や友人、仕事上の知り合いなどに送る、新年の挨拶のためのハガキです。挨拶の言葉を書き、しばしば写真や絵を加えます。新年の十二支の絵は特に人気です。様々な景品が当たるくじ番号付きの専用のハガキを使います。

イラストで くらべる！

Nengajo 年賀状 **VS** Christmas card クリスマスカード

元日に配達されることが
望ましい

クリスマス前の数週間の間に
交換される

Nengajo を英語で説明してみよう

Q. **Do you think the custom of sending *nengajo* is similar to that of sending Christmas cards?**

年賀状を送る習慣って、クリスマスカードを送る習慣と似てると思う？

A. **Yes, I do. Sending them is a good way to keep in touch with relatives and friends. A unique aspect of *nengajo* is that it is desirable that they are delivered exactly on New Year's Day. To ensure such a service, you need to post them by December 25.**

そう思うね。カードを送るのは親戚や友人たちと交信を保つ良い方法だね。年賀状のユニークなところは、年賀状がぴったり元日に配達されることが望ましいってことだね。そんな配達サービスを利用するには、12月25日までに年賀状を投函する必要があるんだ。

🦻 Vocabulary 語句

greeting	名 挨拶		prize	名 景品
postcard	名 ハガキ		keep in touch with ~	～と交信を保つ
relative	名 親戚		desirable	形 好ましい
acquaintance	名 知り合い		deliver	動 ～を配達する
Chinese zodiac sign	（中国の暦法の）十二支（の１つ）		ensure	動 ～を確保する（ここでは、サービスを間違いなく受けるというニュアンス）
contain	動 ～を含む			
lottery number	くじ番号			

Omotenashi
おもてなし

102

What is *omotenashi*?

Omotenashi refers to Japanese-style hospitality. Its basic idea is to treat guests with polite words and attitudes, and offer them heartfelt services from the guests' point of view. The spirit of *omotenashi* developed from the tea ceremony, which emphasizes the host's hospitality and the guests' appreciation to the host.

おもてなしって何だろう？　おもてなしは日本式のホスピタリティを指します。基本的な考えは、お客さんを丁寧な言葉や態度でもてなし、お客さんの観点から心のこもったサービスを行うものです。おもてなしの精神は茶の湯から発達しました。茶の湯は、主人のおもてなしと、客の主人に対する感謝の気持ちを重要視します。

イラストで  くらべる！

Omotenashi おもてなし　VS　Hospitality ホスピタリティ

Q. **I can't get the difference between hospitality and *omotenashi*. Is there any big difference?**

ホスピタリティとおもてなしの差がよくわからないな。何か大きな違いがあるの？

A. **Basically they are similar, but in *omotenashi*, the guests do not request anything and leave everything up to the host. The guests expect some surprise treatment, and the host tries to offer more than expected. In a way, *omotenashi* is an indirect form of communication between the host and the guests.**

基本的には両者は似ているけど、おもてなしでは、客は何も求めずにすべてをホスト側に任せるんだ。客は、何か思いがけないもてなしを期待するし、ホスト側は期待される以上のものを提供しようとするんだよ。ある意味、おもてなしは、客とホスト側との間の間接的なコミュニケーションの様式なんだ。

🚩 Vocabulary 語句

hospitality	名 ホスピタリティ、心のこもったサービス
polite	形 丁寧な
attitude	名 態度、心構え
heartfelt	形 心のこもった
from one's point of view	one の観点から
emphasize	動 ～を重要視する、～を強調する

appreciation	名 感謝の気持ち
leave A (up) to B	A を B に任せる
expect	動 ～を期待する
surprise	形 （形容詞的に）思いがけない
in a way	ある意味
indirect	形 間接的な

103

Itadakimasu
いただきます

What is *itadakimasu*?

Itadakimasu is the phrase we use before a meal. It's a polite way of saying "I'll have it", expressing our gratitude to the food and its producers. After the meal, we say *gochiso-samadeshita*. *Gochiso* means "a good meal", and the whole phrase means "Thank you very much for the delicious meal".

いただきますって何だろう？　「いただきます」は食事の前に使う言い回しです。この言葉は「食べます」を丁寧に言ったもので、食べ物やその生産者に感謝の気持ちを表します。食事の後には「ごちそうさまでした」と言います。ご馳走は「おいしい食事」の意味で、全体の意味は「おいしい食事をありがとうございます」です。

イラストで くらべる！

感謝の気持ちを表す

クリスチャンは神に祈る

Itadakimasu を英語で説明してみよう

Q. **Christians pray to God before and after a meal. Do the phrases the Japanese use also have religious meanings?**

クリスチャンは、食事の前と後に神に祈るけど、日本人が使う言葉も宗教的な意味があるの？

A. **Yes, they do. They are based on Buddhist ideas. The formal prayers are different according to the Buddhist sect, but I think few people know them. Most Japanese say *itadakimasu* and *gochiso-samadeshita* simply as a custom, but starting and ending the meal without these phrases is thought extremely rude.**

うん、あるんだ。それらの言葉は仏教的な考えに基づいているんだ。正式のお祈りも宗派によって違うんだけど、それを知っている人はほとんどいないと思うね。ほとんどの日本人は、単に習慣として「いただきます」や「ごちそうさま」と言うんだけど、これらの言葉を言わずに食事を始めたり終えたりすると、極めて不作法だと思われるよ。

🧧 Vocabulary 語句

phrase	名 言い回し、言葉遣い		pray to 〜	〜に祈る
polite	形 丁寧な		religious	形 宗教的な
express	動 〜を表現する		prayer	名 祈りの言葉
gratitude	名 感謝の気持ち		custom	名 習慣
meal	名 （1回分の）食事		extremely	副 極めて
whole	形 全体の		rude	形 不作法な
delicious	形 おいしい			

104

Sumimasen
すみません

What is *sumimasen*?

Sumimasen is the phrase used when Japanese apologize. It's similar in meaning to "I'm sorry", or "Excuse me", in English. It literally means that something has not finished, implying that the speaker needs to do something to compensate for what he's done. In formal situations, people use *moshiwake gozaimasen*, which means "I have no excuse".

すみませんって何だろう？　「すみません」は日本人が謝罪をするときに使う表現です。この表現は、英語の "I'm sorry" や "Excuse me" と意味が似ています。文字通りの意味は、何かが終わっていない、つまり話者が自分のやったことに対し、何か埋め合わせをする必要があることを示唆します。正式な場においては「申し訳ございません」を用いますが、これは "I have no excuse" の意味です。

イラストで くらべる！

"I'm sorry" や "Excuse me" と
似ている意味

Sumimasen を英語で説明してみよう

Q. **I've noticed Japanese often say, "I'm sorry" when they don't need to apologize. Why is that?**

日本人は謝る必要がないときに、よく "I'm sorry" と言うよね。どうして？

A. **In such a case, they simply mean "Excuse me". Many Japanese often mistranslate the Japanese phrase *sumimasen*, which does mean "I'm sorry", but is also commonly used when people want to get someone's attention or interrupt others. The Japanese language has so many polite expressions, and sometimes it's difficult for Japanese to find equivalent English phrases.**

その場合は単に "Excuse me" の意味だよ。多くの日本人が「すみません」という日本語をしばしば間違えて訳すんだ。「すみません」には、確かに "I'm sorry" の意味があるけど、同時に、人の注意を引いたり、人の話を中断したりしたいときにもよく用いられるんだ。日本語には丁寧な表現が多くて、日本人には、それと同意義の英語表現を見つけるのが難しいときがあるんだよ。

🎎 Vocabulary 語句

phrase	名 言い回し	mistranslate	動 〜を誤訳する
apologize	動 謝罪する（名詞の「謝罪」は apology）	get attention	注意を引く
literally	副 文字通りに	interrupt	動 （人の話などを）中断させる
imply	動 暗示する、示唆する	polite	形 丁寧な
compensate for 〜	〜の埋め合わせをする	equivalent	形 同意義の
formal	形 正式な		

105

Ojigi
お辞儀

What is *ojigi*?

Ojigi is the Japanese way of bowing to greet people. There are three different types of *ojigi*. *Keirei* is the most common bow at 30 degrees. *Eshaku* at 15 degrees is used to greet familiar people. *Saikeirei* at 45 to 90 degrees is used to show your apology or pay respect to deities at rituals.

お辞儀って何だろう？ 　お辞儀は人に挨拶をするときの日本流の頭の下げ方です。お辞儀には 3 種類あります。敬礼は、30 度に体を傾けて行う、最も一般的なお辞儀です。会釈は 15 度で、親しい人たちに挨拶するときに用います。最敬礼は 45 から 90 度で、謝罪の気持ちを示すときか、儀式で神に崇敬の念を表すときに用います。

Ojigi お辞儀　**VS**　Handshake 握手

Ojigi を英語で説明してみよう

Q. People in Western cultures shake hands when greeting. Is it common in Japan?

西洋文化の人たちは、挨拶するときに握手をするけど、日本でも普通？

A. Yes, it is, but handshakes are mainly used when Japanese greet Westerners. Among the Japanese themselves, the bow is still thought appropriate. The handshake indicates both parties are on an equal footing, but in Japan, it is required to greet others appropriately based on their social statuses.

普通だけど、握手は主に、日本人が西洋人に挨拶をするときに使われるね。日本人同士の間では、今でもお辞儀が適切と思われているよ。握手は、両者が対等の立場であることを示すけど、日本では、相手の社会的地位に基づいて適切に挨拶をすることが求められるんだ。

 Vocabulary 語句

bow	名 お辞儀 動 お辞儀をする
greet	動 〜に挨拶をする
common	形 一般的な
at 〜 degrees	（角度が）〜度で
familiar	形 親しい
show one's apology	謝罪の気持ちを示す
pay respect to 〜	〜に崇敬の念を表す
deity	名 （神仏の）神

ritual	名 儀式
shake hands	握手をする（名詞の「握手」は handshake）
appropriate	形 適切な
party	名 関係者
on an equal footing	対等の立場で
appropriately	副 適切に
status	名 地位

106 Kanpai

乾杯

What is *kanpai*?

Kanpai refers to a Japanese-style toast. *Kanpai* literally means to drink up sake from one's cup. It is practiced at the beginning of a party to celebrate auspicious occasions or to pray for people's health. In a *kanpai* ceremony, a designated person delivers a short speech, and then gives a toast.

乾杯って何だろう？　乾杯は日本式の祝杯の上げ方です。乾杯の文字通りの意味は、自分の盃から酒を飲み干すことです。乾杯は、慶事を祝ったり健康を祈ったりする宴席の最初に行われます。乾杯の儀式では、指名を受けた人が短い挨拶をし、その後、乾杯の音頭を取ります。

イラストで くらべる！

Kanpai 乾杯 VS Western toast 西洋の祝杯

Kanpai を英語で説明してみよう

Q. **Is a *kanpai* ceremony derived from a Western toast?**

乾杯の儀式は、西洋の祝杯に由来する？

A. **Yes, it is. The present style of clinking glasses after a toast was introduced into Japan in the mid 19th century, when Japan opened itself to Western countries. It is said that a Japanese original style of *kanpai* is to hold the sake cup high in the air before drinking the sake together.**

そうだよ。乾杯の音頭の後でグラスをカチンと鳴らす様式は、日本が西洋諸国に対して開国した 19 世紀中頃にもたらされたんだ。日本の元々の乾杯は、一緒に飲む前に、盃を高く持ち上げるやり方だったと言われているね。

🎯 Vocabulary 語句

toast	名 祝杯を上げること	designated	形 指名を受けた
drink up ～	～を飲み干す	deliver a speech	スピーチをする
celebrate	動 ～を祝う	give a toast	乾杯の音頭を取る
auspicious	形 めでたい	be derived from ～	～に由来する
occasion	名 出来事	clink	動 （乾杯でグラスを）チンと触れさせる

107

Oshibori
おしぼり

What is oshibori?

Oshibori is a wet hand towel served at restaurants, *izakaya* and other places for customers to wipe their hands before eating and drinking. It is often served warm in winter and cold in summer to make it more refreshing. The custom of serving oshibori originated from Japan's hospitality culture.

おしぼりって何だろう？　おしぼりは、レストランや居酒屋などで、客が食べたり飲んだりする前に手を拭くために出される、湿らせたタオルです。おしぼりは、より爽快に感じるように、冬は温めて、夏は冷やして出すことがよくあります。おしぼりを出す習慣は、日本のおもてなしの文化から生まれました。

Oshibori を英語で説明してみよう

Q. **Can I use an oshibori to wipe my mouth while eating, like a napkin?**

ナプキンみたいに、食事中におしぼりで口を拭いてもいいの？

A. **Well, some people say it is bad manners, but in fact, there are no set rules for using an oshibori, so you can use it as you like. Some people even wipe their face with it, although young people, especially women, might frown upon others doing so.**

えっと、中には無作法と言う人もいるけど、実際には、おしぼりの使い方に決まりはないんだ。だから、自分がやりたいようにして構わないよ。中には、おしぼりで顔を拭く人もいるよ。ただし、若い人、特に女性は他の人がそうすると眉をひそめるかもしれないけどね。

🎎 Vocabulary 語句

wet	形 湿らせた	custom	名 習慣
wipe	動 〜を拭く	originate from 〜	〜から生まれる
serve 〜 warm [cold]	〜を温かく［冷たく］して出す	hospitality	名 おもてなし
		bad manners	無作法
refreshing	形 心身を爽快にするような	frown upon 〜	〜に眉をひそめる

271

108

Daruma
ダルマ

What is daruma?

Daruma is a round doll modeled on a Buddhist monk named Bodhidharma, the founder of Zen. Daruma is regarded as a lucky charm. It has white blank eyes when purchased, and the owner draws in one eye with a wish, and draws in the other when the wish has come true.

ダルマって何だろう？
ダルマは、禅の創始者の菩提達磨という仏僧をモデルにした丸い人形です。ダルマは、幸運のお守りとされています。ダルマは、買ったときには、白い空白の目がありますが、買った人が願いとともに、目を１つ描き入れ、その願いがかなったときに、もう１つの目を描き入れます。

イラストでくらべる！

Daruma ダルマ VS Rabbit's foot ウサギの足

願いがかなったら、もう１つ目を描き入れる

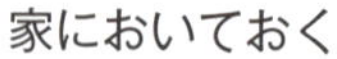

家においておく

持ち歩く

Daruma を英語で説明してみよう

Q. **Do you carry a daruma with you, like a rabbit's foot?**

ダルマは、ウサギの足みたいに持ち歩くものなの？

A. **Well, some people might carry a tiny daruma, but they are usually much bigger and are kept at home until the wish comes true. After your wish has been fulfilled, you take your daruma to a temple that offers a cremation ritual. In the Kanto area, Darumaji Temple in Takasaki is famous for the ritual.**

うーん、極小型のダルマなら持って歩く人もいるかもしれないけど、ダルマはもっと大きくって、普通は、願いがかなうまで家に置いておくものなんだ。願いが成就したら、ダルマを、お焚き上げしてくれるお寺に持って行くんだ。関東地域だと、高崎の達磨寺がその儀式で有名だよ。

😊 Vocabulary 語句

round	形 丸い		owner	名 所有者
be modeled on ～	～をモデルにする		draw in ～	～を描き入れる
			wish	名 願い
Buddhist monk	仏僧、仏教の僧侶		come true	（願いなどが）かなう
founder	名 創始者		rabbit's foot	ウサギの足（西洋でお守りとして身に着ける習慣がある）
lucky charm	幸運のお守り			
blank	形 何も描かれていない		fulfill	動 （願いなどを）成就する
purchase	動 ～を購入する		cremation ritual	お焚き上げ（cremation は「火葬」の意味）

109

Junishi

十二支

What is *junishi*?

Junishi are the twelve signs of the Chinese zodiac, which correspond to years, months and directions. They consist of the mouse, cow, tiger, rabbit, dragon, snake, horse, sheep, monkey, chicken, dog, and boar. The sign of the year is often depicted on New Year's greeting cards to celebrate the coming of New Year.

十二支って何だろう？

十二支は、中国版の十二宮で、年、月、方角などに対応しています。十二支は、子・丑・寅・卯・辰・巳・午・未・申・酉・戌・亥からなります。年賀状には、新年が来るのを祝って、その年の十二支がしばしば描かれています。

Junishi 十二支　**VS**　Western zodiac 西洋の十二宮

Junishi を英語で説明してみよう

Q. Are *junishi* used for fortunetelling, like the Western zodiac?

十二支は、西洋の十二宮みたいに、占いに使われる？

A. Yes, they are, but *junishi* tell people's personality based on their birth year, whereas the Western zodiac is based on people's birth month. What is closer to Western astrology is the Four Pillars of Destiny, which also originated in China. The four pillars refer to people's birth year, month, date and hour.

うん、使われるよ。でも、十二支は人が生まれた年について性格を占うのに対し、十二宮は人が生まれた月に基づいているよね。西洋の占星術に近いのは、四柱推命だね。これも中国発祥だよ。四柱とは、人の生まれた年、月、日、時間のことなんだ。

🟥 Vocabulary 語句

zodiac	名 十二宮（黄道帯を十二等分して、それぞれに近い星座を配置したもの）	celebrate	動 ～を祝う
		New Year	新年、正月
correspond to ～	～に対応する	astrology	名 占星術
		pillar	名 柱
boar	名 イノシシ（中国の十二支では豚）	destiny	名 運命（the Four Pillars of Destiny で「四柱推命」）
depict	動 ～を描く	originate	動 発祥する
greeting card	挨拶状（ここでは、年賀状）		

110

Henro

遍路

What is *henro*?

Henro refers to the pilgrimage to Shikoku's 88 temples related to a Japanese Buddhist saint named Kobodaishi, who lived around the 9th century. People do *henro* to pray for their wishes to come true. The pilgrims are dressed in a white costume, and visit the temples one by one to receive a red seal.

遍路って何だろう？
遍路は、日本人の仏教の高僧、弘法大師にゆかりのある四国八十八箇所への巡礼のことです。弘法大師は９世紀頃の人です。遍路は祈願成就のために行います。巡礼者は白い衣装をまとい、それらのお寺を１つずつ訪れて御朱印をもらいます。

mori2hk/PIXTA（ピクスタ）

Henro を英語で説明してみよう

Q. **Is *henro* similar to pilgrimages in other religions?**

遍路って、他の宗教の巡礼に似ている？

A. **Yes, it is in that they are all aimed at obtaining spiritual healing and benefits. These days, however, more people have *henro* as a form of physical exercise or recreation as well. The 88 temples are popular sightseeing spots visited by many tourists from home and abroad.**

うん、どれも精神的な癒しやご利益を得るのが目的だという点では似ているね。でも最近では、運動や余暇の1つとして遍路を行う人も増えているね。八十八箇所は人気の観光地で、国内外の観光客が多く訪れているよ。

🔴 Vocabulary 語句

pilgrimage	名 巡礼		red seal	ここでは、御朱印
related to ~	~にゆかりのある		be aimed at ~	~を目的としている
saint	名 聖人（ここでは、高僧）		healing	名 癒し
pray for ~	~を祈る		benefit	名 ご利益
wish	名 願い事		physical exercise	運動
come true	（願い事などが）成就する		recreation	名 余暇
pilgrim	名 巡礼者		from home and abroad	国内外からの

Tsunami

津波

What is tsunami?

A tsunami is a series of waves caused by an earthquake occurring under the seafloor. Japan has many earthquakes, and has been repeatedly affected by tsunami. A great earthquake that occurred in the Tohoku Region in 2011 resulted in more than 15,000 deaths, 90 percent of which were due to the tsunami that followed.

津波って何だろう？　津波は、海底で起こる地震によって引き起こされる、連続する波です。日本は地震が多く、津波の影響を繰り返し受けてきました。2011年に東北地方で起こった巨大地震は、15,000人以上の死者を出しましたが、その9割は地震に引き続き起った津波が原因でした。

Tsunami 津波 **VS** **Tidal waves 高潮**

Tsunami を英語で説明してみよう

Q. **Venice in Italy is frequently affected by tidal waves. Is the phenomenon similar to a tsunami?**

イタリアのベニスは頻繁に高潮に襲われているよね。あれは津波の現象と似ているの？

A. **No, it isn't. Tidal waves occur when the sea level is raised by low air pressure. The waves get especially high when it happens at high tide. However, a tsunami occurs when a big earthquake suddenly moves the seafloor, causing the water above to surge upward and fall down.**

いいや、あれは違うね。高潮は、低気圧によって海面が持ち上げられて起こるんだ。それが満潮時に生ずると波が特に高くなるね。でも津波は、大きな地震が海底を突然動かして、その上の水を高くうねらせて引き落とすときに起こるんだよ。

🎎 Vocabulary 語句

a series of ～	連続する、一連の		follow	動 後に続く
earthquake	名 地震		tidal wave	高潮
seafloor	名 海底		low air pressure	低気圧
affect	動 ～に影響を与える、～に害を与える		at high tide	満潮時に
death	名 死亡（件数）		surge	動 （波が）うねる
due to ～	～が原因で		fall down	落ち込む

112 Satoyama

里山

What is *satoyama*?

Satoyama is a border area between mountain foothills and villages. Villagers manage *satoyama* to get firewood and wild vegetables, while *satoyama* provides food and habitats for animals. *Satoyama* have been decreasing due to land development and depopulation in the rural areas, but there's now a movement to preserve *satoyama*.

里山って何だろう？　里山は、山の麓と人里の間の境界地域です。村人は里山を管理し、燃料用材や山菜を調達する一方、里山は動物に食物や生息環境を提供しています。里山は、土地開発や田舎の過疎化によって減少してきましたが、現在、里山を保存する運動が行われています。

イラストで **くらべる！**

Satoyama 里山 **VS** The countryside 田園地方

Satoyama を英語で説明してみよう

Q. **Is *satoyama* like the countryside?**

里山って田園地方と似たようなもの？

A. **They are similar in that both are away from towns and cities. *Satoyama*'s definition has changed with time, and a more recent definition of *satoyama* is the place consisting of forests, rice fields, grasslands, streams and ponds. Well-preserved *satoyama* are now listed by the Japanese government as important cultural landscapes.**

どちらも、町や都市から離れた場所という点においては似ているね。里山の定義もときとともに変わってきたんだ。最近の定義では、林、田んぼ、草地、小川、池などからなる地域を意味しているね。保存状態に優れた里山は、現在、政府によって重要文化的景観としてリスト化されているんだ。

📛 Vocabulary 語句

border area	境界地域	depopulation	名	過疎化
foothills	名 山の麓（通例～s）	preserve	動	～を保存する
manage	動 ～を管理する	definition	名	定義
firewood	名 燃料用材	with time		ときとともに
wild vegetable	山菜	consist of ～		～からなる
habitat	名 生息地	well-preserved	形	保存状態に優れた
land development	土地開発	landscape	名	景観、風景

113 *Tsuyu*

梅雨

What is *tsuyu*?

Tsuyu is the rainy season in Japan. It usually begins in mid-June and lasts around 40 days. *Tsuyu* occurs in most parts of Japan except Hokkaido in the north. When *tsuyu* is over, the temperatures go up, and Japan enters the hot and humid summer season.

梅雨って何だろう？
梅雨は日本の雨期です。梅雨は 6 月中旬に始まり、40 日ほど続きます。梅雨は、北部の北海道を除く日本のほとんどの地域で発生します。梅雨が終わると、気温は上がり、日本は蒸し暑い夏の季節に入ります。

イラストで くらべる！

Tsuyu 梅雨 **VS** **Squall** スコール

しとしと雨が降る

yozo/PIXTA（ピクスタ）

突然激しい雨が降る

Tsuyu を英語で説明してみよう

Q. **In Southeast Asia, they have squalls during the rainy season. Is Japan's rainy season similar?**

東南アジアでは雨期にスコールが発生するよね。日本の梅雨も似ている？

A. **I think it's quite different. We don't have squalls in Japan. In early *tsuyu* we often have drizzling rains, in mid-*tsuyu* we often have hot and sunny days, and toward the end of the *tsuyu* we often have long-lasting torrential rains, which can cause floods and landslides.**

かなり違うと思うね。日本にはスコールはないんだ。梅雨の最初は、シトシトと雨が降ることが多くて、梅雨の中頃には、暑くて晴れの日もしばしばあるね。梅雨の終わりに向けて、長く続く豪雨になることが多くて、洪水や地滑りなどが発生することがあるね。

🟥 Vocabulary 語句

rainy season	雨期
last	動 続く
occur	動 生じる、発生する
be over	終わる
enter	動 （特定の時期や状況などに）入る
hot and humid	蒸し暑い

squall	名 スコール（にわか雨をともなった疾風で熱帯特有の現象）
drizzling rain	シトシトと降る雨
torrential rain	集中豪雨
flood	名 洪水
landslide	名 地滑り

114 Karaoke

カラオケ

What is karaoke?

Karaoke refers to a form of entertainment to enjoy singing to the accompaniment of music provided by a karaoke machine. The lyrics are shown on the display, along with related video clips. People usually enjoy karaoke at the so-called karaoke boxes, which offer soundproof rooms equipped with karaoke machines.

カラオケって何だろう？　カラオケは、カラオケ機器から流れる音楽の伴奏に合わせて、歌って楽しむ娯楽を指します。歌詞はテレビモニター画面に、関連するビデオとともに流されます。日本人は、普通、カラオケ機器を装備した防音室を提供する、いわゆるカラオケボックスでカラオケを楽しみます。

イラストで **くらべる！**

Singing solo 独唱 VS Singing along 合唱

他の人は聞く

1人が歌う

みんなで歌う

Karaoke を英語で説明してみよう

Q. **In Britain, people usually sing along at karaoke, but why do Japanese prefer to sing karaoke solo?**

英国では、普通カラオケで合唱するけど、どうして日本人はソロで歌うのが好きなの？

A. **Japanese tend to avoid standing out in a group, because they think equality, consensus and harmony among the members are important. Karaoke provides a good chance for them to show their individuality by singing their favorite songs. Therefore, it is also considered polite to listen to others' singing.**

日本人は、集団の中で目立つのを避ける傾向があるんだ。集団のメンバー同士での平等、同意、調和が大切だと思っているからね。カラオケは、自分の好きな歌を歌うことで、日本人が個性を見せることができる良い機会を提供してくれるんだ。だから、他の人が歌っているのを聞くのも礼儀だと思われているよ。

🎴 Vocabulary 語句

entertainment	名 娯楽		soundproof room	防音室
accompaniment	名 伴奏		equipped with ～	～を装備した
provide	動 ～を供給する（ここでは、「必要なものを与える」というニュアンス）		sing along	一緒に歌う、合唱する
			sing solo	ソロで歌う、独唱する
lyrics	名 歌詞		equality	名 平等
display	名 テレビモニター		consensus	名 意見の一致
along with ～	～とともに		harmony	名 調和
related	形 関連のある		individuality	名 個性
clip	名 （映画などの）カットされた場面		polite	形 礼儀正しい

115 **Enka**
演歌

What is enka?

Enka is a genre of popular songs established around the 1960s in Japan. Enka songs mostly use the five-note scale and are sung with skillful vibratos. The lyrics are usually sad or serious, featuring lost love or ways of life. Enka singers often wear kimono as a stage costume.

演歌って何だろう？

演歌は、日本で 1960 年代頃に成立した大衆歌のジャンルです。演歌の曲はほとんどが 5 音階のメロディを使っており、こぶしを利かせて歌われます。歌詞は通常、悲しい内容や真剣な内容で、失恋や生き方などを扱っています。演歌歌手は舞台衣装によく着物を用います。

イラストで  くらべる！

Enka 演歌 VS Country music カントリーミュージック

Enka を英語で説明してみよう

Q. **Isn't enka similar to country music in the U.S.?**

演歌って、アメリカのカントリーミュージックに似ていない？

A. **I think so. Both genres are based on national identity, placing emphasis on tradition. Although today, both incorporate the elements of rock music a lot, traditional musical instruments such as the fiddle and steel guitar are used in country songs, and the shamisen and shakuhachi in enka.**

そう思うね。どちらのジャンルも国民性に基づいていて、伝統を重んじるからね。今日では、どちらもロック音楽の要素を多分に入れてはいるけど、カントリー曲だとフィドルとかスティールギター、演歌だと三味線や尺八など、伝統的な楽器も使っているしね。

Vocabulary 語句

genre	名 ジャンル、様式	way of life	生き方、人生観
the five-note scale	５音階のメロディ（ド・レ・ミ・ソ・ラの５つの音からなり、ファとシを使わないメロディ）	stage costume	舞台衣装
		national identity	国民性
skillful	形 高度な技の	place emphasis on ～	～を重んじる
vibrato	名 ビブラート、ここでは、こぶし（小節）	incorporate	動 ～を取り入れる
lyrics	名 歌詞	musical instrument	楽器
serious	形 真剣な		

Jihanki

自販機

What is *jihanki*?

Jihanki means automatic vending machines. There are over 2.5 million vending machines in Japan, which sell various goods including beverages, tickets, cigarettes, and food items. Their annual sales reach nearly 5 trillion yen. Most Japanese commute by train, so vending machines are convenient for them to buy goods on their way.

自販機って何だろう？　自販機は自動販売機のことです。日本には 250 万台以上の自販機があり、飲み物、チケット、タバコ、食品など様々な商品を販売しています。自販機の年間の売り上げは 5 兆円近くに上ります。ほとんどの日本人は電車で通勤しているため自販機は、その途中で何かを買うのに便利なのです。

イラストでくらべる！

Jihanki 自販機　**VS**　Vending machines in America アメリカの自販機

屋外

iStock.com/Brian Niles

室内

Jihanki を英語で説明してみよう

Q. In America, vending machines are usually placed indoors, but in Japan, they are often located outside. Is it secure?

アメリカの自販機は普通、屋内に置いてあるけど日本のはよく外にあるよね。それって安全なの？

A. Yes, it is. Japan's crime rates are very low, and vandalism of outdoor facilities is quite rare. Besides, vending machines are usually located on busy streets, and are often equipped with security alarms and cameras, which I think helps discourage thieves from breaking them open.

安全だよ。日本の犯罪率はとても低くて、屋外の設備に対する破壊行為も極めて少ないからね。それに、自販機は普通、人通りが多い路地に置いてあるし、警報装置や防犯カメラを備えているものも多いから、窃盗犯たちも自販機をこじ開ける気にはならないと思うよ。

Vocabulary 語句

automatic vending machine	自動販売機	secure	形（危害などに対して）安全な
beverage	名 飲み物	crime rate	犯罪率
cigarette	名 タバコ	vandalism	名（公共物の）破壊行為
sales	名 売り上げ（この意味では〜 s）	be equipped with 〜	〜を備えている
commute	動 通勤する	security alarm	警報装置
goods	名 商品（この意味では〜 s）	security camera	防犯カメラ
on one's way	（移動の）途中で	discourage 〜 from doing...	〜が…する気を失わせる
		break 〜 open	〜をこじ開ける

<table><tr><td>117</td><td>

Dagashiya

駄菓子屋

</td></tr></table>

What is *dagashiya*?

Dagashiya are mom-and-pop stores selling various kinds of cheap confections and toys mainly for children. They used to be often found near elementary schools, but due to the decline of Japan's birthrates and increased affluence among Japanese families, there are fewer *dagashiya*. Today *dagashiya* are popular as a tourist attraction.

駄菓子屋って何だろう？　駄菓子屋は主に子供を対象に、様々な種類の安価なお菓子やおもちゃを売る家族経営の店です。昔は小学校の近くでよく見かけたものですが、日本の少子化や、日本の家族が豊かになったことが原因で、駄菓子屋の数は減っています。今では、駄菓子屋は観光の呼び物として人気です。

Dagashiya 駄菓子屋 **VS** **Candy store** キャンディーストア

Dagashiya を英語で説明してみよう

Q. **Are *dagashiya* like candy stores in America?**

駄菓子屋って、アメリカのキャンディーストアみたいなもの？

A. **Yes, they are very similar, although *dagashiya* are seen as a thing of the past. They were most popular during Japan's high economic growth between the 1950s and 1970s. Thanks to the retro boom these days, *dagashiya* and their goods are becoming popular again with people having nostalgia for their childhood.**

そうだね、とてもよく似ているね。ただし、駄菓子屋は過去のものと思われているけどね。駄菓子屋が一番人気だったのは、1950 年代から 1970 年代の日本の高度経済成長期だね。最近のレトロブームのおかげで、子供の頃を懐かしく思う人たちの間で、駄菓子屋や駄菓子屋の商品がまた人気になってきているんだ。

 Vocabulary 語句

mom-and-pop	家族経営の、夫婦だけで運営する	affluence	名 豊かさ	
		tourist attraction	観光の呼び物	
confection	名 菓子	a thing of the past	過去のもの	
toy	名 おもちゃ	high economic growth	高度経済成長	
due to ～	～が原因で			
elementary school	小学校（英国では primary school）	retro	形 レトロの	
		nostalgia	名 ノスタルジア	
birthrate	名 出生率			

Juku

塾

What is juku?

Juku are private schools that provide Japanese elementary and junior high school students with extra education to complement school education. Meanwhile, the schools that help senior high school students and graduates to prepare for entrance examinations for universities are *yobiko*. There are more than 50,000 juku and *yobiko* across Japan.

塾って何だろう？ 塾は、学校教育を補完するための追加教育を日本の小学生や中学生に提供する私学です。一方、高校生や高校卒業生に対し、大学入試の準備を手伝う学校は予備校になります。塾と予備校は全国で約 5 万校あります。

イラストで **くらべる！**

Entrance examination 入試 **VS** **The Significant Six** 6つの要素

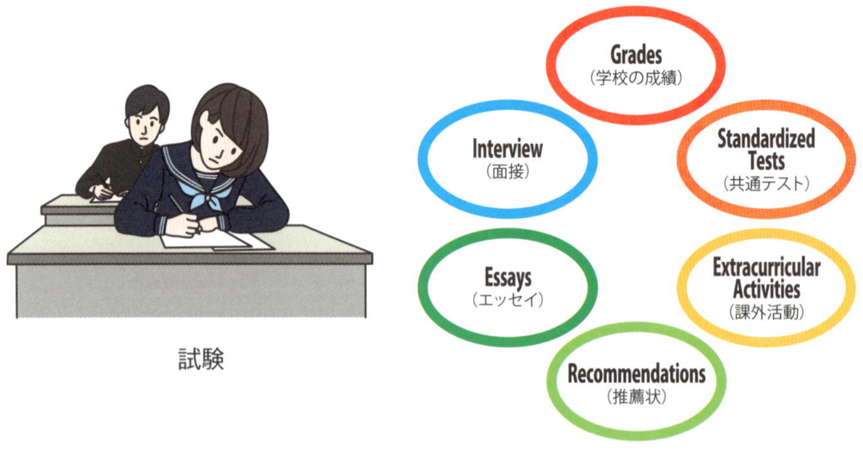

試験

Juku を英語で説明してみよう

Q. In America, there are fewer such schools. Why do so many Japanese students go to juku or *yobiko*?

アメリカにはそのような学校はあまりないな。どうして多くの日本の生徒が塾や予備校に通うの？

A. Japanese school education emphasizes equality among students, so it is not enough for those aiming at prestigious higher schools. Also, admission to high schools and universities is mostly decided by the scores of the entrance examinations, so many students want to be better prepared by going to such schools.

日本の学校教育は生徒間の平等を重視しているんだ。そのため、一流の学校への進学を目指す生徒たちには不十分なんだ。それに、中高や大学への入学は、たいてい、入学試験の点数によって決められるので、多くの生徒がそのような学校に通ってしっかり準備したいと思うんだよ。

🧧 Vocabulary 語句

provide A with B	A に B を提供する
elementary school	小学校
junior high school	（日本の）中学校
extra education	追加教育
complement	動 ～を補完する
senior high school	（日本の）高校
graduate	名 卒業生
prepare for ～	～の準備をする
entrance examination	入学試験（米国の大学入学資格は、学校の成績、エッセイ、推薦状、課外活動、共通テスト、面接の６つの要素、**The Significant Six** によって審査される）
emphasize	動 ～を強調する
equality	名 平等
aim at ～	～を目指す
prestigious	形 一流の
admission	名 入学
be prepared	準備が整っている

119

Shushin-koyo

終身雇用

What is *shushin-koyo*?

Shushin-koyo is the lifetime employment system practiced by Japan's major companies. In the system, the company guarantees its employees jobs until their retirement in return for the employees' strong loyalty to the company. It has long helped Japanese companies to secure skilled workers, while providing job security.

終身雇用って何だろう？　終身雇用は日本の大手企業で行われている雇用制度です。この制度では、従業員の企業への強い忠誠心と引き換えに、企業が従業員に雇用を退職時まで保証します。この制度は、長い間、日本の企業における優秀な人材の確保を助ける一方、安定した雇用を供給してきました。

イラストで くらべる！

Take leave 一時帰休 **VS** **Layoff** 一時解雇

ある程度補償あり

Shushin-koyo を英語で説明してみよう

Q. In America, layoffs are common during economic downturns. Are they common in Japan, too?

アメリカでは、不景気になると一時解雇がよく行われるけど、日本でもそうなの？

A. The layoff system is not common in Japan, although companies might ask the workers to take leave with compensation. In an economic downturn, it is more common for companies to call their employees for voluntary early retirement with increased allowance or to reduce the amount of new recruitment.

一時解雇制度は日本では一般的ではないね。企業が労働者にある程度の補償をして一時帰休をお願いすることはあるけどね。不景気のときには、従業員に退職金を上乗せして早期自主退職を促すか、新規採用を控えるほうが一般的だな。

Vocabulary 語句

lifetime	形 生涯の
guarantee A B	A に B を保証する
retirement	名 退職
in return for 〜	〜と引き換えに
loyalty to 〜	〜に対する忠誠
secure	動 〜を確保する
job security	安定した雇用、雇用確保
layoff	名 一時解雇（アメリカやカナダなどで採用されている制度で、不況時に就労期間が短い者から一時解雇し、長く働いている者から再雇用するもの）
downturn	名 景気の悪化
take leave	休暇を取る（ここでは、賃金の一部を補償して休業させる「一時帰休制度」を指す）
compensation	名 補償
call A for B	A に B を呼びかける
voluntary	形 自主的な
allowance	名 ここでは、退職金
recruitment	名 採用、求人

120

Kenkoku-kinen-no-hi

建国記念の日

What is Kenkoku-kinen-no-hi?

Kenkoku-kinen-no-hi is the National Foundation Day on February 11, one of Japan's 16 national holidays. This day commemorates a legendary enthronement of Japan's first emperor, the Emperor Jinmu, in 660 BC. As a national holiday, it is aimed at promoting patriotism among the Japanese people.

建国記念の日って何だろう？

建国記念の日は2月11日で、日本にある16の休日の1つです。この日は、日本の初代天皇である神武天皇の紀元前660年における伝説的な即位を記念するものです。国民の祝日として、日本国民の愛国心を育む目的があります。

Kenkoku-kinen-no-hi 建国記念の日 **VS** **The Fourth of July** アメリカの独立記念日

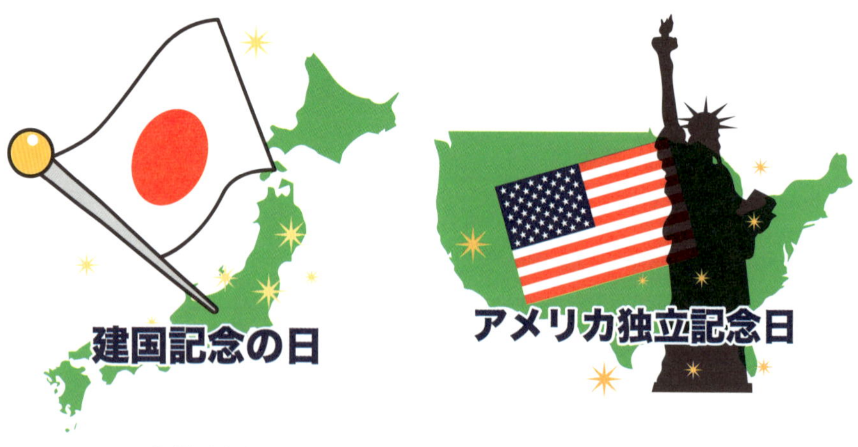

Kenkoku-kinen-no-hi を英語で説明してみよう

Q. **Is Kenkoku-kinen-no-hi similar to the Fourth of July in America?**

建国記念の日って、アメリカの独立記念日に似ている？

A. **Yes, it is in that both commemorate the beginning of the nation. However, the enthronement of the Emperor Jinmu is more of a legend than a historical fact, so there are mixed opinions about this day. Some people say the day comparable to the Fourth of July is the Emperor's birthday.**

そうだね、どちらも国の始まりを記念する点においてはね。でも、神武天皇の即位は、史実というより伝説なんだ。だから、この日に関しては意見も様々だね。アメリカの独立記念日にあたる日は天皇誕生日だと言う人もいるよ。

🟥 Vocabulary 語句

the National Foundation Day	建国記念の日
national holiday	国民の祝日
commemorate	動 〜を記念する
legendary	形 伝説的な
enthronement	名 即位
be aimed at 〜	〜を目的とする
promote	動 〜を育む、〜を促進する
patriotism	名 愛国心
the Fourth of July	（アメリカ合衆国の）独立記念日（1776 年 7 月 4 日。**Independence Day** あるいは、**July Fourth** とも）
legend	名 伝説
mixed	形 （争点などが）混合した
comparable to 〜	〜に匹敵する

121

Honne and Tatemae
本音と建前

What are *honne* and *tatemae*?

Honne is a person's true feelings, and *tatemae* is polite behavior shown in public. The Japanese often use them to maintain harmonious interpersonal relationships. For example, even when people want to say "no", they often reply ambiguously by saying "That's difficult". Such a response is considered more polite in Japan.

本音と建前って何だろう？　本音は本当の気持ち、建前は人前での礼儀正しい態度です。日本人は、協和的な人間関係を保つために、本音と建前をよく使います。例えば、「嫌です」と言いたくても、「それは難しいですね」と曖昧な返答を多々します。このような返答は、日本ではより礼儀正しいものとされています。

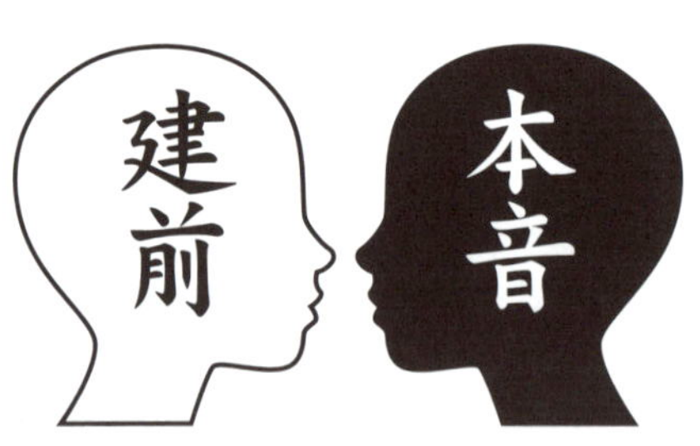

Tatemae を英語で説明してみよう

Q. **Isn't *tatemae* similar to a white lie in English?**

建前って、英語のホワイト・ライに似ていない？

A. **Yes, it is, but white lies are used only for personal matters. In contrast, tatemae is used even in business meetings. In such a case, both parties clearly understand the message behind the tatemae. In Japan, how you convey your message is often more important than the message itself.**

うん、似ているね。でも、ホワイト・ライは個人的なことだけに使われるよね。それとは対照的に、建前は商談においても使われるんだ。そんな場合は、建前の裏にあるメッセージを双方が明確に理解しているんだ。日本では、メッセージそのものよりも、そのメッセージの伝え方のほうが大事なときも多いんだよ。

🟥 Vocabulary 語句

polite	形 丁寧な、礼儀正しい		white lie	儀礼的なうそ（例えば、もらった贈り物が気に入らなくても、相手を傷つけないように、I like it. などのように答えること）
behavior	名（他人に対する）態度			
maintain	動 ～を保つ			
harmonious	形 協和的な、仲の良い			
interpersonal relationship	人間関係		business meeting	商談
reply	動 返答する		party	名（契約などの）当事者、関係者
ambiguously	副 曖昧に			

Q. **Why do many Japanese avoid saying "yes" or "no" clearly?**

多くの日本人はどうして、「イエス」か「ノー」かはっきり言うのを避けるの？

A. **Since the Japanese place emphasis on group consensus, they tend to avoid situations where they might have to make decisions as individuals. In negotiations, for example, they say they will discuss the matter among themselves and then decide. The slow decision making and ambiguous answers also help alleviate the negative effect of refusal when the answer is "no". This is important for Japanese who tend to make much of harmonious relationships.**

日本人は集団でのコンセンサスを重要視するから、個人的に意思決定をしなければならないかもしれない状況を避けたがるんだ。例えば、交渉なんかで、みんなで話し合って決めますとか言うよね。また、時間がかかる意思決定や曖昧な返答は、答えが「ノー」だったときに、拒否することの悪影響を和らげてくれる効果があるんだ。このことは、円満な人間関係を大切にする傾向がある日本人にとって、重要なことなんだ。

Vocabulary 語句

place emphasis on ～	～を重視する	refusal	名 拒否
make a decision	意思決定をする	make much of ～	～を大切にする
negotiation	名 交渉	harmonious	形 円満な
ambiguous	形 曖昧な	influence	名 影響
negative effect	悪影響	Confucianism	名 儒教

Q. Why do Japanese often ask about other people's ages?

日本人はどうして人の年齢を聞くことが多いの？

A. One reason is the influence of Confucianism. Confucianism emphasizes respect for people older than oneself. For example, younger people are expected to use polite words when they talk to seniors to show respect. Knowing others' ages provides important behavioral criteria for many Japanese. Another reason is that Japanese culture is different with regard to privacy. Japanese society strongly emphasizes harmonious interpersonal relationships. This harmony is reinforced by sharing each other's personal information. Asking about people's ages in Japan, therefore, is not considered so rude.

1つの理由は儒教の影響だね。儒教は自分より年上の人に対する敬意を大切にするんだ。例えば、若い人たちは、年上の人たちに話すときには、敬意を示すために丁寧な言葉を使うのが当然とされている。相手の年齢を知っておくのは、多くの日本人にとって、大切な行動基準を示してくれるんだ。もう1つの理由は、プライバシーに関して日本文化は異なっていることだね。日本の社会は円満な人間関係をとても重視する。この円満さはお互いの個人情報を共有することによって補強されるんだよ。だから、日本においては、人の年齢を聞くのはさほど失礼だとは思われていないんだ。

Vocabulary 語句

emphasize	動 ～を重視する	with regard to ～	～に関して
respect	名 敬意	reinforce	動 ～を補強する
polite	形 丁寧な	rude	形 失礼な
behavioral criteria	行動基準		

Wabi and sabi

わびさび

122

What is wabi and sabi?

Wabi and sabi are important elements that constitute the Japanese sense of beauty. Wabi refers to deliberate simplicity in daily living, and sabi refers to the appreciation of the old and faded. They are emphasized in the tea ceremony, haiku poetry, and many other aspects of Japanese culture.

わびさびって何だろう？

わびとさびは、日本人の美的感覚を構成する重要な要素です。わびは日常生活における意図的な簡素さを指し、さびは古くてさびれたものに美を見出すことです。わびさびは、茶の湯や俳句など、日本文化の多くの側面で重視されています。

Shiyali/PIXTA（ピクスタ）

Wabi and sabi を英語で説明してみよう

Q. My dictionary translates sabi as a patina. What do you think?

自分の辞書は、さびを a patina（趣）と訳しているけど、どう思う？

A. Well, a patina refers to the attractive appearance created by long use of an object. In that sense, it may be close to the concept of sabi. However, I think wabi and sabi are unique in that they're connected to Buddhist philosophy, which emphasizes transience and imperfection in things.

そうだな、patina は、ある物を長く使い続けたことから生まれる魅力的な外見を意味するけど、その意味においては、さびの概念に近いだろうね。でも、わびさびは、物事の無常や不完全さを強調する仏教哲学と結びついているところが独特だと思うね。

Vocabulary 語句

element	名 要素		aspect	名 側面
constitute	動 ～を構成する		patina	名 （長い間に備わった）趣
sense of beauty	美的感覚		unique	形 独特な
deliberate	形 意図的な		be connected to ～	～と結びついている
simplicity	名 簡素さ		philosophy	名 哲学
appreciation	名 美を見出すこと		transience	名 無常
the old and faded	古くてさびれたもの		imperfection	名 不完全さ
emphasize	動 ～を強調する			

Q. **Can you tell me about Buddhist philosophy a little more in detail?**

仏教の思想についてもう少し詳しく聞かせてくれない？

A. **Buddhism teaches nothing lasts forever. This teaching resulted in the Japanese sense of beauty found in the transience of life. A good example is the Japanese love of cherry blossoms. They burst into bloom at once, and the petals fall in a very short period of time. They indicate that no matter how beautiful they are, they are imperfect because they are destined to wither away soon, just like our lives. That's why we need to treasure each and every moment encountered.**

仏教は、永遠に続くものは何１つない、と教えるけど、この教えの結果、日本人は、無常観に美意識を見出すようになったんだ。その良い例が、日本人が桜の花を好きなことだね。桜の花は一気に花開いて、短い期間に花びらが散ってしまう。このことが示すのは、どんなに桜の花が美しくても、桜の花は不完全で、すぐにしおれる運命にあるということ。僕らの命のようにね。だからこそ、僕らは遭遇する１つ１つの瞬間を大切にする必要があるんだ。

Q. **Is there any place you recommend that I visit to better appreciate wabi and sabi?**

わびとさびをよりよく理解するために訪れる場所でお勧めは？

A. **It might be a good idea to visit Japanese gardens. I recommend Ryoanji in Kyoto. Its garden is a typical dry landscape garden, with 15 rocks simply placed on white sand. Another good place is Saihoji Temple also in Kyoto. Its garden is a stroll style, and is covered with moss all over, so the temple is also called a moss temple. Moss grows slowly taking many years and is thought to be a symbol of antiquity and tranquility. It really represents the world of wabi and sabi.**

日本庭園を訪れるのが良いと思うね。京都の龍安寺はお勧めだよ。そこの庭園は典型的な枯山水で、15 の石が白い砂の上に素朴においてあるんだ。また別の良い場所が西芳寺で、これも京都だね。そこの庭園は回遊式で、あたり一面が苔に覆われているんだ。そのため、お寺は苔寺とも呼ばれている。苔は何年もかけてゆっくり成長するから、古色と静寂の象徴とされているんだ。まさに、わびさびの世界を表しているね。

🎎 Vocabulary　語句

burst into bloom	開花する		encounter	動 ～に遭遇する
petal	名 花びら		dry landscape garden	枯山水
imperfect	形 不完全な		stroll style	回遊式の
be destined to do ～	～する運命にある		moss	名 苔
wither away	しおれる		antiquity	名 古色（古びた様子）
treasure	動 ～を大事にする		tranquility	名 静寂

123

Manga
マンガ

What is manga?

Manga refers to Japanese-style comics. The prototype of manga is said to be picture scrolls made in the 12th century, but manga as we know it today emerged after World War II. Manga covers a wide range of topics and is popular among people of all ages.

マンガって何だろう？　マンガは、日本式のコミック誌のことです。マンガの原型は、12 世紀頃に作られた絵巻物と言われますが、今日の私たちが知っているようなマンガが現れたのは、第二次世界大戦後です。マンガは、幅広い話題を扱っており、あらゆる年齢層の人たちに人気です。

イラストで  くらべる！

Manga マンガ **VS** **Western comic** 西洋のコミック誌

あらゆる年齢層に人気

子供向け

Manga を英語で説明してみよう

Q. **How do you compare manga with Western comics?**

マンガと西洋のコミック誌を比べるとどう？

A. Comics are usually for children, but manga are read by adults as well. Manga dealing with social issues became popular among young factory workers in cities in the 1950s. Since then, manga has developed into a medium covering politics, economy, hobbies, and many other interesting topics.

コミック誌は通常子供向けだよね。でもマンガは、大人の人たちにも読まれているんだ。1950 年代に、社会問題を扱うマンガが都会の若い工場労働者たちの間で人気になったんだ。それ以後、マンガは、政治、経済、趣味などの人の興味を引く題材を扱うメディアに発達していったんだ。

🎎 Vocabulary 語句

comic	名 コミック誌	a wide range of ~	幅広い~
prototype	名 原型	people of all ages	あらゆる年齢層の人たち
a picture scroll	絵巻物	develop into ~	~へと発達する
emerge	動 現れる	medium	名 伝達手段（複数形は media）
cover	動 ~を扱う、~をカバーする		

Q. **Why are manga read from right to left?**

マンガはどうして右から左へと読み進むの？

A. **Traditionally, the Japanese language is written vertically, and lines move from right to left, so naturally book pages are turned from left to right as opposed to Western books. This tradition is maintained in Japanese language school textbooks, literary works, newspapers and magazines. And manga is no exception. However, in the case of academic books, which may contain foreign words, mathematical formulas and music scores, Japanese is usually written horizontally like English to make it easier to read, and pages are turned from right to left.**

伝統的に、日本語は縦書きで、行が右から左へと進むんだ。だから自然と、本も左から右へとページをめくるんだ。西洋の本とは反対にね。この伝統は、学校の国語の教科書、文学作品、新聞、雑誌などで維持されている。マンガも例外ではないんだ。でも、外国語や数式や楽譜などを含むことがある学術書の場合は、読みやすくするために、日本語を英語のように横書きにして、ページも右から左へとめくるようにしてあるのが普通なんだ。

Q. I saw Japanese written horizontally from right to left. When is it used?

右から左に横書きにしてある日本語を見たことあるけど、どんなときに使うの？

A. As a matter of fact, it's vertically-written Japanese with line breaks made after each single character. So, it is written only in a single horizontal line from right to left. This style is often used for name boards of temples, and was frequently used in newspaper headlines in the old days, but it has mostly disappeared. Meanwhile, writing Japanese horizontally from left to right began with scholars of Dutch in the Edo Period, and gradually became common in the fields of science.

実を言うと、それは縦書きの日本語で、一文字ごとに改行が入っているんだよ。だから、右から左へと横１行のみでしか書かないんだ。この書き方はお寺の額によく使われているし、昔は新聞の見出しに頻繁に使われていたけど、ほとんど見かけなくなったね。一方で、左から右への日本語の横書きは、江戸時代に蘭学者によって始められて、次第に科学の分野で普通に用いられるようになったんだ。

🔴 Vocabulary 語句

vertically	副 縦向きに	horizontally	副 横向きに
as opposed to ~	～とは反対に	line break	改行
maintain	動 ～を維持する	name board	額、看板
academic book	学術書	newspaper headline	新聞の見出し
mathematical formula	数式	scholars of Dutch	蘭学者
music score	楽譜		

124

Kokkai

国会

What is *kokkai*?

Kokkai, or the National Diet, is Japan's legislature. It is the highest organ of state power. It consists of the House of Representatives and the House of Councilors. Diet members are directly elected by the nation. The Diet chooses the Prime Minister, who organizes the Cabinet, Japan's administrative branch.

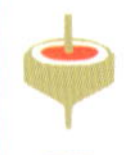

国会って何だろう？
国会は、日本の立法府です。国会は、国権の最高機関で、衆議院と参議院からなっています。国会議員は国民の直接選挙で選ばれます。国会は首相を選び、首相は、日本の行政府である内閣を組織します。

Japan's Prime Minister 日本の首相 **VS** **President in the U.S.** 米国の大統領

日本の首相：国会議員　　　　　米国の大統領：国会議員ではない

国会議事堂：
国会が開催される建物

アメリカ合衆国議会議事堂：
国議会の議事堂

Kokkai を英語で説明してみよう

Q. **How is Japan's Prime Minister different from the President in the U.S.?**

日本の首相は米国の大統領とどう違う？

A. **Japan has the parliamentary cabinet system, in which the Prime Minister and more than half of the Cabinet members must be Diet members. But in the U.S., the administrative branch and the legislative branch are clearly separated, so the President and the Cabinet members are not the Parliament members.**

日本は議院内閣制を採っているため、首相および閣僚の半数以上が国会議員でなければならないんだ。ところが米国では、行政府と立法府が明確に分かれているから、大統領も閣僚も国会議員ではないんだ。

🟥 Vocabulary 語句

the (National) Diet	（日本の）国会（英国では **Parliament**、米国では、**Congress** と呼ばれる）	Diet member	国会議員
legislature	名 立法府	elect	動 ～を（選挙で）選ぶ
organ	名 機関	Prime Minister	首相、内閣総理大臣
state power	国権	organize	動 ～を組織する
the House of Representatives	（日本の）衆議院	the Cabinet	内閣
the House of Councilors	（日本の）参議院	administrative branch	行政府
		the parliamentary cabinet system	議院内閣制

Q. How are Diet members elected?

国会議員はどのようにして選ばれるの？

A. As for the House of Representatives, Japanese people aged 25 or over are eligible for candidacy. Currently it has 465 seats. The term is four years, but the House of Representatives is subject to dissolution by the Cabinet, so the election is held when the term is over or when it is dissolved. As for the House of Councilors, candidates must be at least 30 years old. Currently it has 242 seats, and the term is six years. The election is held every three years to re-elect half of the members.

衆議院に関しては、25 歳以上の日本人に立候補する資格がある。現在、定数は 465 議席。任期は 4 年だけど、衆議院は内閣によって解散させられることもあるから、選挙は任期が切れたときか解散されたときに行われる。参議院に関しては、候補者は 30 歳以上。現在定員は 242 議席＊で、任期は 6 年。選挙は 3 年ごとに行われて半数が改選されるんだ。

＊2018 年時点の議席数。2022 年より 248 議席。

Q. How is the Prime Minister chosen?

総理大臣はどのようにして選ばれるの？

A. Each party designates one candidate for the Prime Minister, and the leader of each party usually becomes the party's candidate. The Prime Minister is selected by majority vote in both the House of Representatives and the House of Councilors, but when their results are different, the decision by the House of Representatives takes priority. Theoretically, the Prime Minister can be chosen from either house, but so far, there's been no Prime Minister from the House of Councilors.

各党が総理大臣の候補を１人指名するけど、普通は各党の党首がその党の候補者になる。総理大臣は、衆議院と参議院において投票して多数決で選ばれるけど、両院の結果が違っている場合、衆議院の決定が優先される。理論的には、総理大臣はどちらの院からも選ばれる可能性があるけど、参議院から選ばれた総理大臣はまだ存在しないね。

🎎 Vocabulary 語句

be eligible for ～	～の資格がある		candidate	名 立候補者
candidacy	名 立候補		re-elect	動 ～を改選する
term	名 任期		designate	動 ～を指名する
be subject to ～	～の対象である		majority vote	投票による多数決
dissolution	名 解散		take priority	優先する
election	名 選挙		theoretically	副 理論上は
dissolve	動 ～を解散させる			

Jieitai

125 自衛隊

What is *jieitai*?

Jieitai is Japan's self-defense forces. Although the present Japanese constitution renounces war and possession of military forces, it does not deny the Japanese people's rights to defend themselves. Under such an interpretation, Japan has the Self-Defense Forces, which are aimed only at defending Japan and the Japanese people.

自衛隊って何だろう？　自衛隊は日本の自己防衛のための部隊です。現行の日本国憲法は、戦争と軍隊の保持を放棄していますが、日本人が自らを防衛する権利を否定するものではありません。そのような解釈の下で、日本には、日本国および日本国民を防衛することのみを目的とした自衛隊があります。

イラストで くらべる！

Jieitai 自衛隊 VS Military forces 軍隊

目的：日本国、および日本国民を守ることのみ

iStock.com/flySnow

Jieitai を英語で説明してみよう

Q. **What's the difference between the Self-Defense Forces and military forces in other countries?**

自衛隊と他の国の軍隊ってどう違うの？

A. Under international laws, self-defense forces are regarded as military forces, but because of the Japanese constitution, the Japan Self-Defense Forces can use force only when Japan is attacked by military forces of other countries. Today, there's an argument for changing the constitution to expand their roles.

国際法の下では、自己防衛のための部隊は軍隊と見なされているけど、日本国憲法があることで、日本の自衛隊が武力を行使するのは、日本が他国の軍隊から攻撃を受けたときだけに限られているんだ。今では、自衛隊の役割を拡張するために憲法を改正することが議論されているよ。

Vocabulary 語句

self-defense forces	自己防衛のための部隊（「自衛隊」の固有名詞としては、the Japan Self-Defense Forces と呼ばれる）
present	形 現行の
constitution	名 憲法
renounce	動 ～を放棄する
possession	名 保持、所有
military force	軍隊

deny	動 ～を否定する
defend	動 ～を防衛する
interpretation	名 解釈
be aimed at ～	～を目的としている
force	名 武力
be attacked	攻撃を受ける
argument	名 議論
expand	動 ～を拡大する

Q. How does the Japanese constitution stipulate the renunciation of war?

日本国憲法は、戦争放棄についてどのように規定しているの？

A. It stipulates it in Article 9. It consists of two paragraphs:

Aspiring sincerely to an international peace based on justice and order, the Japanese people forever renounce war as a sovereign right of the nation and the threat or use of force as means of settling international disputes.

In order to accomplish the aim of the preceding paragraph, land, sea, and air forces, as well as other war potential, will never be maintained. The right of belligerency of the state will not be recognized.

日本国憲法はその第９条において規定している。９条は２つの項からなっているんだ。
日本国民は、正義と秩序を基調とする国際平和を誠実に希求し、国権の発動たる戦争と、武力による威嚇又は武力の行使は、国際紛争を解決する手段としては、永久にこれを放棄する。
前項の目的を達するため、陸海空軍その他の戦力は、これを保持しない。国の交戦権は、これを認めない。

Vocabulary 語句

stipulate	動 ～を規定する	sovereign right	国権
renunciation	名 放棄	threat	名 威嚇
aspire to do ～	do しようと希求する	as means of ～	～の手段として
justice	名 正義	dispute	名 紛争
order	名 秩序	accomplish	動 ～を達する

Q. **So, what interpretation justifies the existence of the SDFs?**

それで、どんな解釈が自衛隊の存在を正当化しているの？

A. **The last part of the first paragraph says "as means of settling international disputes", so the article leaves room for interpretation that in case Japan is attacked or its territory is invaded by a foreign power despite no existence of international disputes, the Japanese can defend themselves and their territories militarily. Under this interpretation, however, if Japan admits the existence of international disputes over a specific issue, the SDFs cannot be involved in it. That's one reason why the government wants to amend the constitution.**

最初の項の最後は、「国際紛争を解決する手段としては」と述べているよね。だから、この条文では、国際紛争が存在していないにもかかわらず、外国勢力によって日本が攻撃を受けたり、日本の領土が侵略されたりした場合は、日本人は軍事的に日本国民、およびその領土を防衛できる、と解釈できる余地を残してあるんだ。ただし、この解釈では、もし特定の問題について日本が国際紛争の存在を認めると、自衛隊はそれに関与できないんだ。これが、政府が憲法を改正しようとしている1つの理由なんだ。

🎎 Vocabulary 語句

war potential	戦力	militarily	副 軍事的に
belligerency	名 交戦状態	admit	動 ～を認める
leave room for ～	～の余地を残す	issue	名 問題
territory	名 領土	amend	動 （憲法などを）改正する
invade	動 ～を侵略する		

INDEX

本書で扱った 125 のトピックを日本語の五十音順に並べたリストです。

● 著者　**江口裕之**（えぐち・ひろゆき）

1957 年、長崎県生まれ。CEL 英語ソリューションズ最高教育責任者、通訳案内士（英語）、日本文化研究家。国立北九州高専化学工学科卒業後、プロのミュージシャンとして東京を本拠地に全国で演奏活動を展開。その後、通訳・翻訳家および通訳案内士として活躍。2001 年 1 月、東京に英語学校の CEL 英語ソリューションズを設立。2009 〜 13 年、NHK E テレ語学番組「トラッドジャパン」講師。2017 年 4 〜 6 月 NHK ラジオ語学番組「短期集中！3 か月英会話：めざせ！スポーツボランティア」講師。著書に『英語で語る　日本事情 2020』(共著、The Japan Times)、『外国人と街歩き英会話　日本を伝えるフレーズ 2100』(The Japan Times) などがある。

本書へのご意見・ご感想は下記 URL までお寄せください。
http://www.jresearch.co.jp/contact/

カバーデザイン	喜田里子
本文デザイン / DTP	有限会社ギルド
本文イラスト	山本のり（のりしろ・デザイン舎）
ナレーション	Howard Colefield
	Karen Haedrich
ダウンロード音声制作	一般財団法人 英語教育協議会（ELEC）

英語でガイド！
世界とくらべてわかる　日本まるごと紹介事典

平成 30 年（2018 年）9 月 10 日　　初版第 1 刷発行
令和 7 年（2025 年）8 月 10 日　　　第 3 刷発行

著　者	江口裕之
発行人	福田富与
発行所	有限会社　Ｊリサーチ出版
	〒 166-0002　東京都杉並区高円寺北 2-29-14-705
	電話 03(6808)8801 （代）　FAX 03(5364)5310　編集部 03(6808)8806
	http://www.jresearch.co.jp
	Twitter 公式アカウント　@Jresearch_　　https://twitter.com/Jresearch_
印刷所	（株）シナノ　パブリッシング　プレス

ISBN978-4-86392-400-0　禁無断転載。なお、乱丁・落丁はお取り替えいたします。